REVISE FOR ADVANCED PE FOR OCR AS

Dave Carnell
John Ireland
Ken Mackreth
Sarah van Wely

Endorsed by OCR

Heinemann Educational Publishers
Halley Court, Jordan Hill, Oxford OX2 8EJ
Part of Harcourt Education

Heinemann is the registered trademark of
Harcourt Education Limited

First published 2004

09 08 07 06 05
10 9 8 7 6 5 4 3

British Library Cataloguing in Publication Data is available
from the British Library on request.

ISBN 0 435 58315 8

Typeset by J & L Composition, Filey

Printed in the UK by Scotprint

Acknowledgements
The publishers would like to thank the following for the use of logos: Disability Sport England on p.125; Dragon Sport on p.101; English Institute of Sport on p.123; Sports coach UK on p.125; Sport England on p.123; Sportsmatch on p.126; TOP Sport on p.101; Women's Sports Foundation on p.125; UK Athletics on p.124; UK Sport on p.123; Youth Sport Trust on p.100.

All exam questions reproduced with kind permission of OCR.

The publishers would like to thank the following for permission to reproduce photographs:
Empics p.52, p.60 (top and bottom); Camera Press p.111; Action Images p.114.

Every effort has been made to contact copyright holders of material reproduced in this book. Any omissions will be rectified in subsequent printings if notice is given to the publishers.

Tel: 01865 888058 www.heinemann.co.uk

Contents

Introduction

This book has been produced specifically for students revising for OCR's AS Physical Education (PE) specification. It contains information on all the topics that are examined in:

Unit 2562

- Section A: Application of anatomical and physiological knowledge to improve performance
- Section B: Acquiring and performing movement skills

Unit 2563

- Contemporary studies in physical education

This book follows the same structure as *Advanced PE for OCR, AS* also published by Heinemann and contains the key information that you need to know for your examination.

At the beginning of each unit and each chapter, you will find overview charts with tick boxes, which you can use to help plan your revision as well as checking your progress. If you are not satisfied with your level of knowledge and understanding of a particular topic or chapter, then you can revisit those areas.

The book includes certain features to help you:

Need to know more?

This provides cross-references to *Advanced PE for OCR, AS* if you need further information on a topic.

Key words

These are emboldened in the text and listed separately. These are the key words and terms that you need to know.

Hot tips

These are designed to give you exam help and advice.

Exam practice

At the end of each chapter, you will find a section of exam style questions. When you have completed your revision for a chapter, you should answer the questions, which will enable you to test your knowledge and understanding as well as practising your exam technique. When you have completed the questions, check your answers with those provided at the end of the book. Compare your marks with 'How did you do?' which gives advice on your next course of action. In some cases, this may involve giving yourself a pat on the back, or it may involve finding out which areas you did not do well in and doing some more work on them.

Whilst this book will help you in your revision for your examinations, there is no substitute for planning and spending time and effort putting that plan into action. Establish your revision schedule and the learning method most suited to you. Use this revision book to support your plan.

Good luck!

Unit 1: Anatomy and physiology

Unit overview

Unit 1: Anatomy and physiology

- Chapter 1: Joints and movement ☐
- Chapter 2: Muscles and movement ☐
- Chapter 3: Mechanics, motion and movement ☐
- Chapter 4: Part I – Cardiovascular system ☐
- Chapter 4: Part II – Control of blood supply ☐
- Chapter 5: Respiratory system ☐

Tick the box when you are satisfied with your level of knowledge and understanding within each chapter.

Chapter 1 **Joints and movement**

Chapter overview

Chapter 1: Joints and movement

1 Classification of joints ☐

2 Synovial joints ☐

3 Types of synovial joints ☐

4 Anatomical terminology and movement ☐

NEED TO KNOW MORE?

For further information on joints and movement, see pp. 4–18 in *Advanced PE for OCR, AS.*

Tick the box when you are satisfied with your level of knowledge and understanding for each topic within this chapter.

1 Classification of joints

Joints are where two or more bones **articulate**. Joints are classified according to the movement they permit.

Structural class of joint	Function/movement	Example
Fibrous	Fixed/immovable.	Cranium, sacrum and coccyx.
Cartilaginous	Slightly movable.	Vertebrae.
Synovial	Freely movable.	Shoulder, hip.

KEY WORDS

Joints

Articulate

Appendicular skeleton

Axial skeleton

There are two divisions of the skeleton:

- **appendicular.** These are freely movable joints of the upper and lower limbs and their girdles that join to the axial skeleton. Its function is to provide a framework for muscle attachment and movement.
- **axial.** More commonly, immovable and slightly movable joints that form the long axis of the body including the cranium, spine and ribcage. Its function is to protect, support and carry other body parts.

HOT TIPS

In your examination, you would never be asked to label a skeleton, but you would be expected to know the bones that articulate at the following joints: wrist, radio-ulnar, elbow, shoulder, spine, hip, knee and ankle.

2 Synovial joints

Synovial joints have four common distinguishing features.

Feature	Structure	Function
Articular/hyaline cartilage	Glassy-smooth cartilage that is quite spongy. It covers the ends of the bones at the joint.	• To prevent friction between the articulating surfaces of the bones at the joint. • To absorb compression placed on the joint and protect the bone ends from being crushed.
Two-layered joint capsule	The outer layer is a tough fibrous layer called the fibrous capsule. The inner layer is the synovial membrane that covers all the internal joint surfaces except for the articular cartilage.	• To strengthen the joint so that the bones are not pulled apart. • To secrete synovial fluid.
Synovial fluid	A slippery fluid the consistency of egg-whites that is contained within the joint cavity.	• To reduce friction between the articular cartilages. • To nourish the articular cartilage. • To rid the joint of any waste debris.
Ligament	A band of strong fibrous tissue.	• To connect one bone to another bone.

Other common structures specific to individual joints include the following:

Feature	Structure	Function
Bursa (bursae)	Flattened fibrous sac lined with synovial membrane containing a thin film of synovial fluid.	Prevent friction at sites where ligaments, muscles, tendons or bones might rub together.
Meniscus (menisci)	A wedge of white fibrocartilage (tough/flexible) that improves the fit between adjacent bone ends.	Increases joint stability and reduces wear and tear to joint surfaces.
Pad of fat	A fatty pad located between capsule, bone or muscle.	Increases joint stability and reduces friction between joint surfaces.

HOT TIPS

Remember, the starting point for these movements is the anatomical position. If you get confused with a joint movement, freeze your body in the position you want to describe and return to the anatomical position to work out what movement has happened at that joint.

3 Types of synovial joints

Synovial joints are classified into six groups according to the shape of their articulating surfaces:

- ball and socket = hip and shoulder
- hinge = knee, elbow and ankle
- pivot = radio-ulnar, tibia-fibula and atlas/axis
- condyloid = wrist
- gliding = vertebrae
- saddle = thumb.

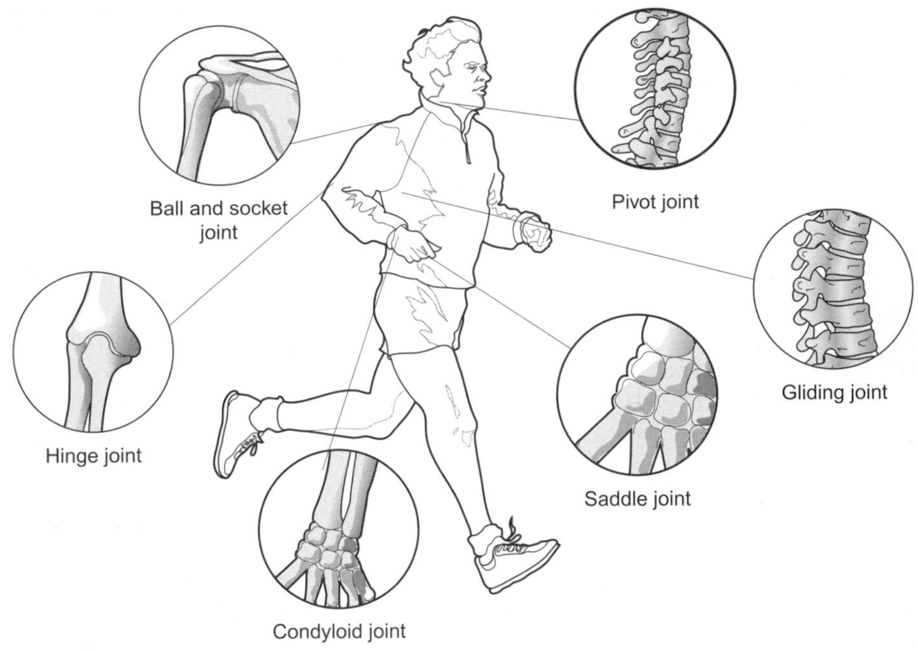

Fig. 1.01 The six types of synovial joint found in the body.

KEY WORDS

Anatomical position

Medial

Lateral

4 Anatomical terminology and movement

- **Anatomical position:** an upright standing position with the head, shoulders, chest, palms of the hands, hips, knees and toes all facing forwards.
- **Medial:** situated in or movement towards the middle of the body.
- **Lateral:** situated in or movement towards the outside of the body.

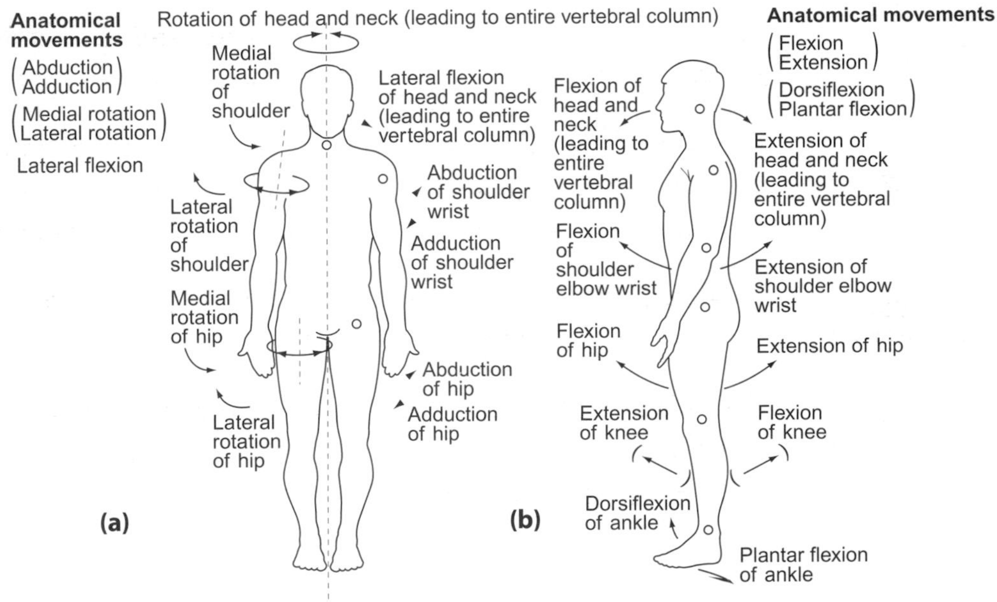

Fig. 1.02 Summary of the anatomical movement of the synovial joints of the body. The anatomical position is shown (a) from the front and (b) from the side.

The table below summarizes the movements of the major joints.

Joint	Possible movements
Wrist	• Flexion and Extension • (Abduction and Adduction) • (Circumduction)
Radio-ulnar	• Rotation i.e. Pronation and Supination
Elbow	• Flexion and Extension
Shoulder	• Flexion and Extension • Horizontal flexion and Horizontal extension • Abduction and adduction • Rotation • Circumduction
Spine	• Flexion and extension • Lateral flexion • (Rotation)
Hip	• Flexion and extension • Abduction and adduction • Rotation • (Circumduction)
Knee	• Flexion and extension
Ankle	• Dorsiflexion and plantar flexion

Here are some tips for remembering important facts that may appear in the exam:

Flexion always moves forwards and extension backwards. The knee joint is the only exception to this rule where flexion moves the lower leg backwards and extension moves the lower leg forwards.

Remember horizontal flexion and horizontal extension – the fingers are already pointing at the horizon at the start of the movement.

Abduction – think about when something is taken away.

Adduction – think about the word 'add' in maths, when you always add one number to another.

Bending the spine from side to side is lateral flexion.

Remember the difference between pronation and supination by how you carry a bowl of soup (supination) in the palm of your hand.

To remember rotation and circumduction movements, imagine a pen is being held at the end of a body part. If it is rotation, the pen will draw a dot; if it is circumduction, the pen will draw a circle.

Plantar flexion of the ankle occurs when you point your toes, so remember '**p**' for **p**oint and for **p**lantar flexion.

Always answer joint movement in table form to help you identify clearly the joint movement taking place. Always name the joint that is moving for example, elbow flexion.

CHECK !

Go back to the overview diagrams on pp. 1 and 2. If you are satisfied with your knowledge and understanding, tick off the sections that you have revised so far. If you are not satisfied, then revisit those sections and refer to the pages in the 'Need to know more?'

Exam practice

Examination questions for joints and movement are incorporated within Chapter 2, 'Muscles and movement', p. 14, as they would be in an examination.

Chapter 2 **Muscles and movement**

Chapter overview

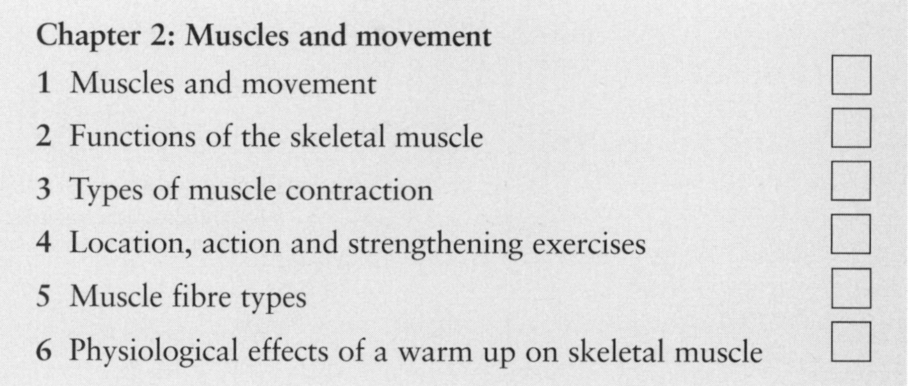
Chapter 2: Muscles and movement

1 Muscles and movement ☐
2 Functions of the skeletal muscle ☐
3 Types of muscle contraction ☐
4 Location, action and strengthening exercises ☐
5 Muscle fibre types ☐
6 Physiological effects of a warm up on skeletal muscle ☐

Tick the box when you are satisfied with your level of knowledge and understanding for each topic within this chapter.

For further information on muscles and movement, see pp. 19–39 in *Advanced PE for OCR, AS*.

1 Muscles and movement

Skeletal muscle attaches to and moves the skeleton and is also called voluntary muscle as it is under our conscious control.

Skeletal muscle

2 Functions of the skeletal muscle

Muscles perform one of three roles when producing movement. For example, the upward phase of a biceps curl shown in Figure 2.01.

Remember these muscles are arranged in pairs, so whatever movement one muscle can do, it will have a partner muscle that can reverse that movement.

Agonist/prime mover

Antagonist

Fixator

Muscle	Function	Explanation
Biceps brachii	**Agonist/prime mover**	The biceps brachii muscle pulls the lower arm upwards when its insertion moves towards its origin.
Triceps brachii	**Antagonist**	The triceps brachii muscle relaxes or lengthens to allow the biceps brachii muscle to shorten.
Trapezius	**Fixator**	The trapezius muscle applies a force to stabilise the scapula in order to hold the origin of the biceps brachii still.

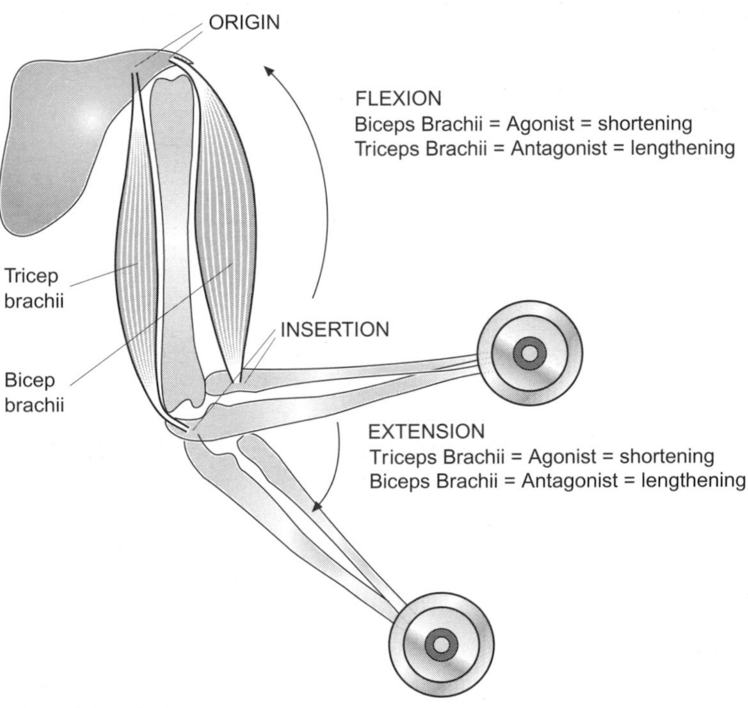

Fig. 2.01 Origin and insertion of the biceps, Tricep brachii showing antagonistic muscle action of the elbow.

Antagonistic muscle action
Insertion
Origin

Muscles are attached to bone in at least two places and cross at least one joint by tendons.

The tendon that remains relatively fixed during a muscular contraction is called the **origin**.

The tendon that tends to move towards the origin during a muscular contraction is called the **insertion**.

Muscles can only pull. They cannot push and must cross a joint to be able to move that joint.

Muscles are arranged in pairs to bring about paired movement. For example, biceps brachii causes elbow flexion, whilst triceps brachii causes elbow extension.

The pairing of muscles is termed **antagonistic muscle action**. As one muscle shortens to produce movement, the paired muscle lengthens to allow the movement to take place.

Isotonic

Isometric

3 Types of muscle contraction

Isotonic

- Muscle exerts a force while changing length.
- If the muscle is lengthening, it is called an **eccentric** contraction.
- If the muscle is shortening, it is called a **concentric** contraction.

Isometric

- The muscle is exerting force but there is no change in muscle length.

Function linked to type of muscular contraction

Joint analysis exam questions are always in the form of a table or a diagram.

Function	Movement/tension	Contraction
Agonist	Shortening (under tension)	Concentric
Antagonist	Lengthening (under tension)	Eccentric
Fixator	No change (but under tension)	Isometric

Eccentric assumes the muscle is lengthening but acting as a brake to help control a movement.

4 Location, action and strengthening exercises

All tables term the antagonist eccentric contractions in respect to them lengthening, but they are only truly eccentric if the muscle is under tension and acting as a brake to help control the movement.

It is essential that you can apply the movement classification using examples or when interpreting diagrams/tables. See Figure 1.02 in Chapter 1. Examples of diagrams from past examination question papers are included to give you an idea of what to expect.

Wrist joint

Action	Function agonist	Type of contraction	Function antagonist	Type of contraction	Strengthening exercise
Flexion	Wrist flexors	Concentric	Wrist extensors	Eccentric	Wrist curl
Extension	Wrist extensors	Concentric	Wrist flexors	Eccentric	Reverse wrist curl

Radio-ulnar joint

Action	Function agonist	Type of contraction	Function antagonist	Type of contraction	Strengthening exercise
Pronation	Pronator teres	Concentric	Supinator	Eccentric	Dumb-bell curl downward phase
Supination	Supinator	Concentric	Pronator teres	Eccentric	Dumb-bell curl upward phase

Elbow joint

Action	Function agonist	Type of contraction	Function antagonist	Type of contraction	Strengthening exercise
Flexion	Biceps brachii	Concentric	Triceps brachii	Eccentric	Bicep curl
Extension	Triceps brachii	Concentric	Biceps brachii	Eccentric	Tricep extension

Shoulder joint

Action	Function agonist	Type of contraction	Function antagonist	Type of contraction	Strengthening exercise
Flexion	Anterior deltoid	Concentric	Triceps brachii	Eccentric	Bicep curl
Extension	Posterior deltoid	Concentric	Biceps brachii	Eccentric	Tricep extensions
Medial rotation	Subscapularis teres major	Concentric	Infraspinatus teres minor	Eccentric	
Lateral rotation	Infraspinatus teres minor	Concentric	Subscapularis teres major	Eccentric	
Abduction	Medial deltoid	Concentric	Latissimus dorsi	Eccentric	Back press
Adduction	Latissiumus dorsi	Concentric	Medial deltoid	Eccentric	Chin ups
Horizontal flexion	Pectoralis major	Concentric	Trapezius	Eccentric	Bench press
Horizontal extension	Trapezius	Concentric	Pectoralis major	Eccentric	Seated row

continued

Spine

Action	Function agonist	Type of contraction	Function antagonist	Type of contraction	Strengthening exercise
Flexion	Rectus abdominus	Concentric	Erector spinae group	Eccentric	Crunches
Extensions	Erector spinae group	Concentric	Rectus abdominus	Eccentric	Back extensions
Lateral flexion	External/Internal obliques (left or right)	Concentric	Opposite (left or right) external/internal obliques	Eccentric	Broomstick twists

Hip joint

Action	Function agonist	Type of contraction	Function antagonist	Type of contraction	Strengthening exercise
Flexion	Iliopsoas	Concentric	Gluteus maximus	Eccentric	Sit ups
Extensions	Gluteus maximus	Concentric	Iliopsoas abdominus	Eccentric	Bent knee hip extensions
Medial rotation	Gluteus medius/ minimus	Concentric	Gluteus maximus	Eccentric	
Lateral rotation	Gluteus maximus	Concentric	Gluteus medius/ maximus	Eccentric	
Abduction	Gluteus medius/ minimus	Concentric	Adductor group	Eccentric	Side hip raises
Adduction	Adductor group	Concentric	Gluteus medius/ minimus	Eccentric	Floor hip adductions

Knee joint

Action	Function agonist	Type of contraction	Function antagonist	Type of contraction	Strengthening exercise
Flexion	Biceps femoris, semitendinosus, semimembranosus	Concentric	Rectus femoris, vastus: lateralis, medialis, intermedius	Eccentric	Leg curls

Action	Function agonist	Type of contraction	Function antagonist	Type of contraction	Strengthening exercise
Extension	Rectus femoris, vastus: lateralis, medialis, intermedius	Concentric	Biceps femoris, semitendinosus, semimembranosus	Eccentric	Dumb-bell squat

Ankle joint

Action	Function agonist	Type of contraction	Function antagonist	Type of contraction	Strengthening exercise
Dorsiflexion	Tibialis anterior	Concentric	Gastrocnemius and soleus	Eccentric	Toe taps
Plantar flexion	Gastrocnemius, and soleus	Concentric	Tibialis anterior	Eccentric	Toe raises

See *Advanced PR for OCR, AS*, pp. 23–32 for diagrams for each of the joints tables.

5 Muscle fibre types

Muscle fibres are the long cylindrical muscle cells held together in bundles that make up an individual muscle, there are three types.

	Slow oxidative fibres (SO; type I)	Fast oxidative glycolytic fibres (FOG; type IIa)	Fast glycolytic fibres (FG; type IIb)
Structural variations			
Colour	Red	Red to pink	White (pale)
Size	Small	Intermediate	Large
No. of mitochondria	Many	Many	Few
No. of capillaries	Many	Many	Few
Myoglobin concentration	High	High	Low
Glycogen stores	Low	Intermediate	High
Functional variations			
Contractile speed	Slow	Fast	Fast
Contractile strength	Low	Intermediate	High
Fatigue resistance	High	Moderate	Low
Aerobic capacity	High	Moderate	Low
Anaerobic capacity	Low	High	High
Location	e.g. gastrocnemius of marathon runner	e.g. gastrocnemius of 1500m runner	e.g. gastrocnemius of 110m hurdler
Best suited activities	e.g. endurance type activities	e.g. activities involving walking, running and sprinting	e.g. speed/power type activities

Fast twitch

Muscle fibre

Slow twitch

Slow twitch	Fast twitch
Designed for aerobic work.	Designed for anaerobic work.
Uses O_2 to produce a small amount of force.	Does not require O_2 and produces a large amount of force.
Slow speed of contraction.	Fast speed of contraction.
Fatigue resistant; for example, a marathon runner.	Fatigues quickly, for example, a sprinter or shot putter.

6 Physiological effects of a warm up on skeletal muscle

A warm up is light aerobic exercise that takes place prior to exercise. It normally includes some light exercise to elevate the heart rate, some mobilizing exercises for the joints, some stretching exercises for the muscles, and some rehearsals of the skills to follow.

- Increased strength of contraction due to improved elasticity of muscle fibres.
- Faster speed of contraction due to increased speed of nerve impulse to muscle.
- Faster speed and relaxation of contraction due to higher muscle temperature.
- Increased speed of strength of contraction due to improved co-ordination between antagonistic pairs, due to a reduction in muscle viscosity.
- Increased speed and strength of contraction due to increase in enzyme activity in warmer muscles.
- Reduced risk of injury, despite an increase in speed of strength of contraction, due to increase in blood flow and oxygen to muscles.

CHECK !

Go back to the overview diagrams on pp. 1 and 7. If you are satisfied with your knowledge and understanding, tick off the sections that you have revised so far. If you are not satisfied, then revisit those sections and refer to the pages in the 'Need to know more?'

Exam practice

1 To develop strength in specific muscle groups, a performer must undertake specific exercises.

(a) The tables and diagrams below show two exercises commonly used to develop strength in targeted muscle groups. Apply your knowledge of movement analysis to complete the tables. Write your answers in the tables. (5 marks)

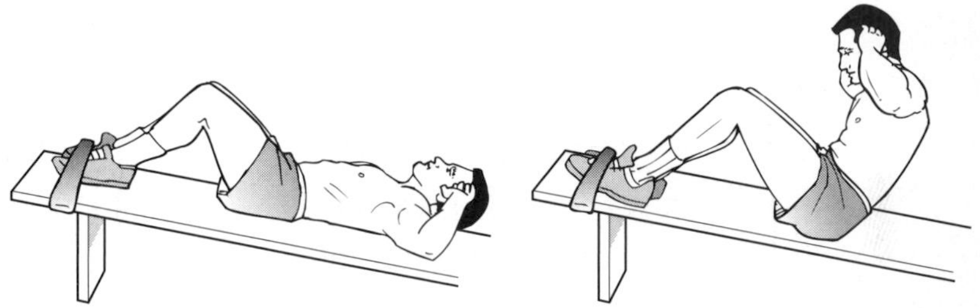

Joint	Joint type	Articulating bones	Movement produced	Prime mover
Spine	Cartilaginous/gliding	Vertebrae		

Joint	Joint type	Articulating bones	Movement produced	Prime mover
Elbow				Biceps brachii

(b) During the downward phase of the biceps curl, the role of the biceps brachii alters. Identify the type of contraction being performed by the biceps brachii during the controlled downward phase and explain how its role has changed. (2 marks)

(c) Identify the predominant muscle fibre type being used during the biceps curl to produce maximum lift (one repetition, maximum weight). Give one structural and one functional characteristic of the fibre type. (3 marks)

2 The figure below shows a swimmer performing the front crawl stroke.

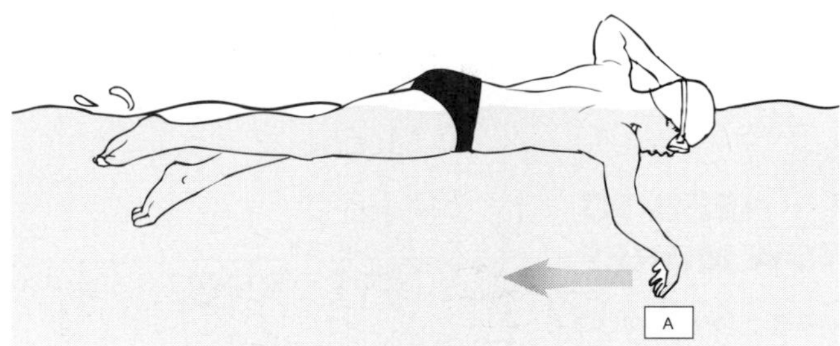

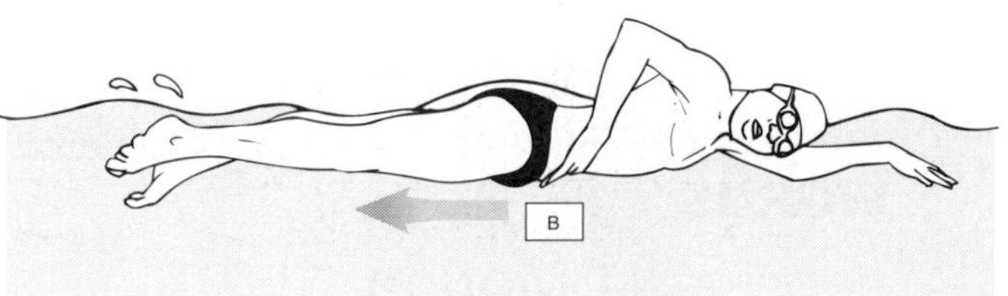

(a) Identify the joint type, articulating bones, and the agonist (prime mover) causing extension at the shoulder joint during the propulsion phase (from A to B). (3 marks)

(b) The shoulder joint is commonly classed as a synovial joint. Identify four structural features of the shoulder joint and explain their function during physical activity. (4 marks)

3 The figure below shows an athlete driving from the blocks at the start of a 60-metre sprint race.

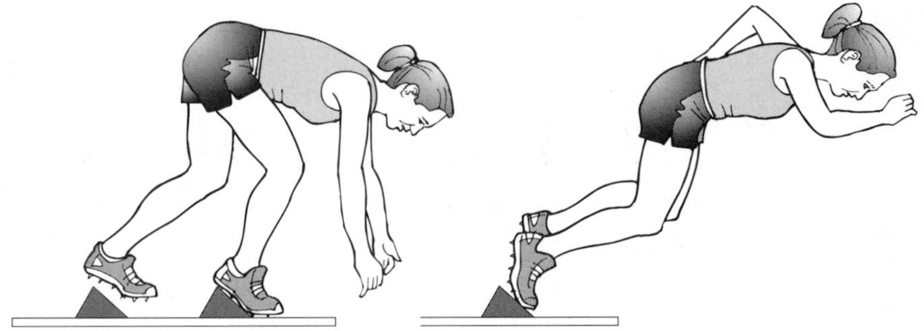

Identify the joint type, articulating bones, and the agonist (prime mover) causing the extension of the hip joint as the athlete drives from the blocks. (3 marks)

Now go to p. 141 to check your answers.

Chapter 3 **Mechanics, motion and movement**

Chapter overview

Chapter 3: Mechanics, motion and movement

1 Motion ☐

2 Force ☐

3 Newton's Laws of Motion ☐

4 Centre of mass ☐

NEED TO KNOW MORE?

For further information on mechanics, motion and movement, see pp. 42–51 in *Advanced PE for OCR, AS*.

Tick the box when you are satisfied with your level of knowledge and understanding for each topic within this chapter.

KEY WORDS

Linear motion

Angular motion

Axis of rotation

1 Motion

Motion is movement and there are three types of motion.

Linear motion

This is when a body moves in a straight or curved line with all parts moving the same distance, direction and speed for example a tobogganist in a straight line or a shot putt in a curved line.

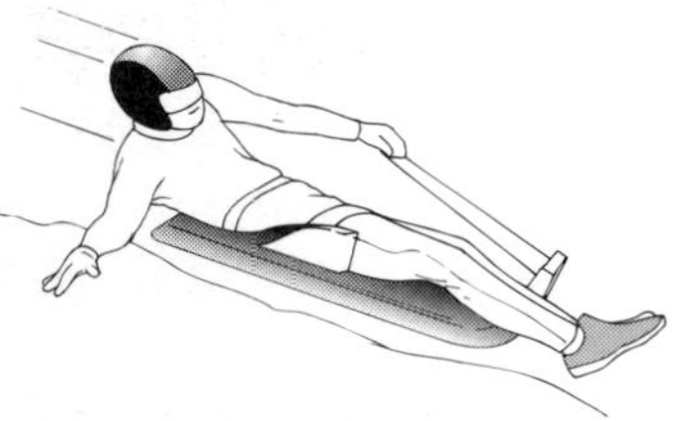

Fig. 3.01 Linear motion of a tobogganist in a straight line.

Angular motion

This is when a body, or part of a body, moves in a circle, or part of a circle, around a particular point called the **axis of rotation.** For example, the shoulder joint in swimming or the whole body around the high bar in gymnastics.

Fig. 3.02 Axis of rotation; the whole body around the high bar.

General motion

This is a combination of linear and angular motion.

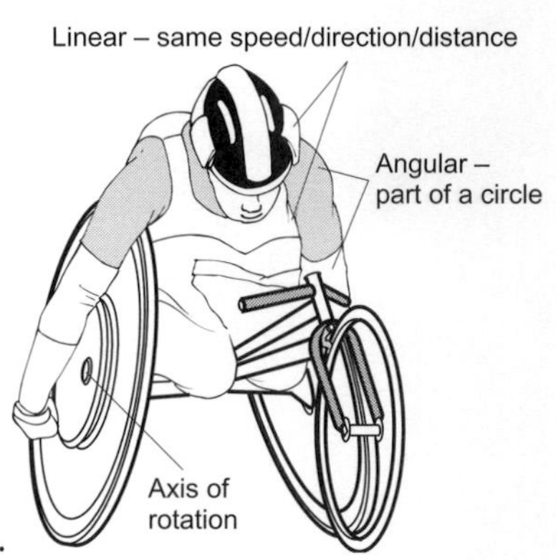

Fig. 3.03 General motion.

For further information on motion, see pp. 42–5 in *Advanced PE for OCR, AS.*

2 Force

Force is a push or pull that alters or tends to alter the state of motion of a body. It can:

- cause a body at rest to move
- cause a moving body to change direction, accelerate, or decelerate
- change an object's shape.

KEY WORDS

Force

Without force, there can be no motion.

The extent of the resulting motion is dependent upon:

- where the line of application of the force is applied
- the size of the force applied = Newton's Second Law of Motion
- the direction in which the force is applied = Newton's Second Law of Motion
- the link between motion and force is explained by a knowledge of Newton's Laws.

3 Newton's Laws of Motion

First Law of Inertia

'A body continues in a state of rest or uniform velocity unless acted upon by an external force.'

Second Law of Acceleration

'When a force acts upon an object, the rate of change of momentum is proportional to the size of the force and takes place in the direction in which the force acts.'

Third Law of Reaction

'For every action there is an equal and opposite reaction.'

The netballer will continue in a state of rest (standing) unless acted upon by an external force (muscular force applied to the ground).

1st law

When the netballer applies force to the ground the accceleration is proportional to the size of the force (height jumped with a greater force applied to the ground).

2nd law

For every action (netballer pushes the ground directly down with her feet) there is an equal and opposite reaction (the ground exerts an equal force upwards).

3rd law

GA

Fig. 3.04 Newton's Law of Motion applied to jumping.

For further information on Newton's Laws of Motion, see pp. 45–7 in *Advanced PE for OCR, AS*.

4 Centre of mass

The **centre of mass** is the point at which the body is balanced in all directions, or where all the mass could be considered to be concentrated.

Centre of mass

The centre of gravity is continually changing and can lie within or outside the mass of the body.

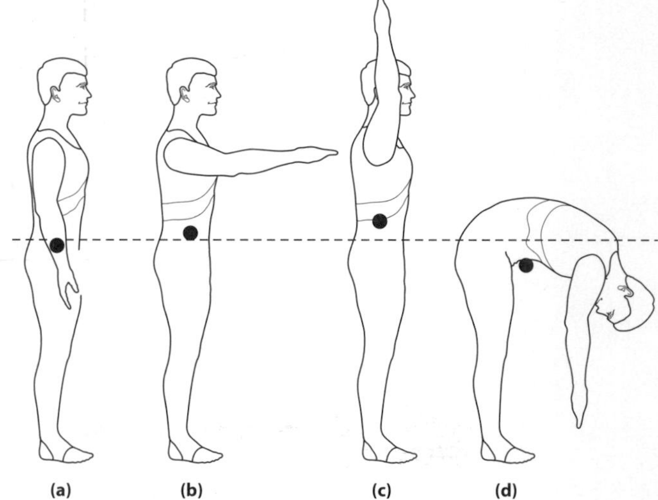

Fig. 3.05 Centre of mass changing within (a,b,c) and outside (d) the mass of the body.

Stability

Stability

Stability is how difficult it is to disturb a body from a balanced position.

Stability is dependent upon four principles.

Line of gravity

1 Position of athlete's centre of mass.
2 Athlete's base of support (feet).
3 Position of athlete's **line of gravity**.
4 Mass of the athlete.

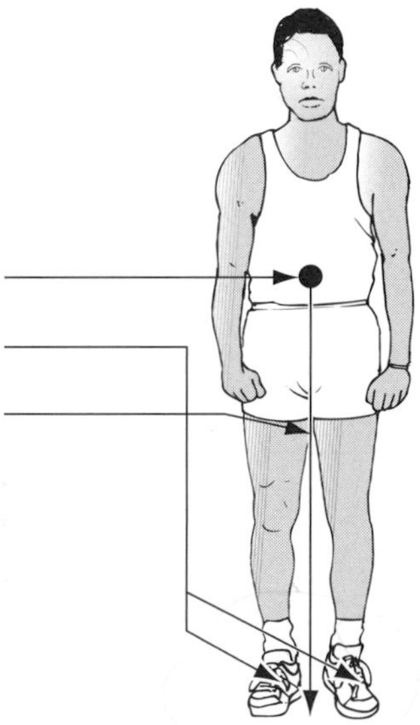

The line of gravity is a line extending from the centre of mass vertically down to the ground.

Fig. 3.06 Male athlete showing position of centre of mass.

Stability is increased when:

- the centre of mass is within the base of support
- the centre of mass is lower
- there are wider/more bases of support
- the line of gravity is shorter and within the base of support
- the mass is greater and lower.

Relationship between centre of mass and application of force

The direction of the application of a force in relation to the centre of mass determines whether the motion of a body is linear or angular.

Direct force = linear motion

A force whose line of application passes through a body's centre of mass will cause the resulting motion to be linear.

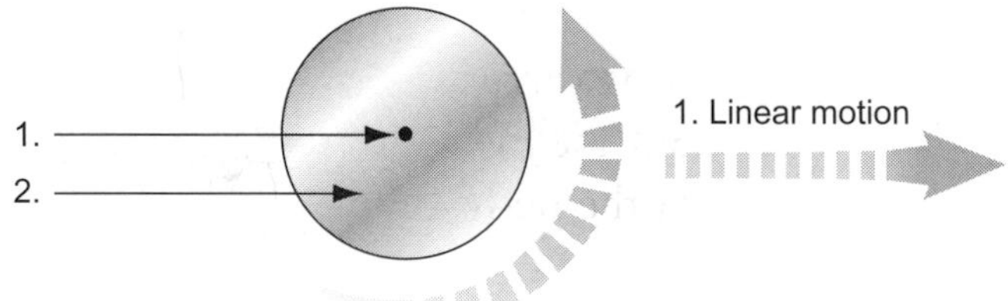

Fig. 3.07 Force – line of application.

Direct force

Eccentric force

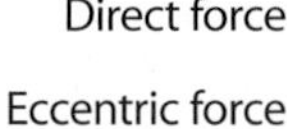

Eccentric force = angular motion

A force whose line of application passes outside the centre of mass of a body causing the resulting motion to be angular (rotation/spin).

CHECK !

Go back to the overview diagrams on pp. 1 and 16. If you are satisfied with your knowledge and understanding, tick off the sections that you have revised so far. If you are not satisfied, then revisit those sections and refer to the pages in the 'Need to know more?'

Exam practice

1 Knowledge of force can be beneficial when analysing physical activities. Using practical examples, explain how the size of force, direction of force and position of application of the force can affect performance. (3 marks)

2 Using examples from your practical activities, explain how knowledge of Newton's Laws of Motion would improve performance. (3 marks)

3 The application of force is essential to maximize performance. Using a physical activity of your choice, explain how an understanding of force can improve performance. (4 marks)

4 The figure below shows a gymnast performing a headstand and a handstand.

With reference to the centre of mass, explain why a headstand is an easier balance to hold than a handstand. (3 marks)

Now go to p. 143 to check your answers.

Chapter 4 Part I: **Cardiovascular system**

Chapter overview

Chapter 4: Part I: Cardiovascular system

1 Review of heart structure and function ☐

2 Heart's conduction system linked to the cardiac cycle ☐

3 Resting heart rate – volumes and definition ☐

4 Heart rate response to exercise ☐

5 Heart rate regulation and control ☐

NEED TO KNOW MORE?

For further information on the cardiovascular system, see pp. 52–72 in *Advanced PE for OCR, AS.*

Tick the box when you are satisfied with your level of knowledge and understanding for each topic within this chapter.

1 Review of heart structure and function

'Aerobic work' refers to exercise that relies predominantly on the use of oxygen to supply the energy for prolonged performance. 'Aerobic system' refers to three distinct systems: the heart, vascular and respiratory system, which closely interact to ensure a constant distribution of oxygen to the muscles during exercise.

HOT TIPS

Examination questions often require you to combine information from the three systems, particularly the heart and vascular systems.

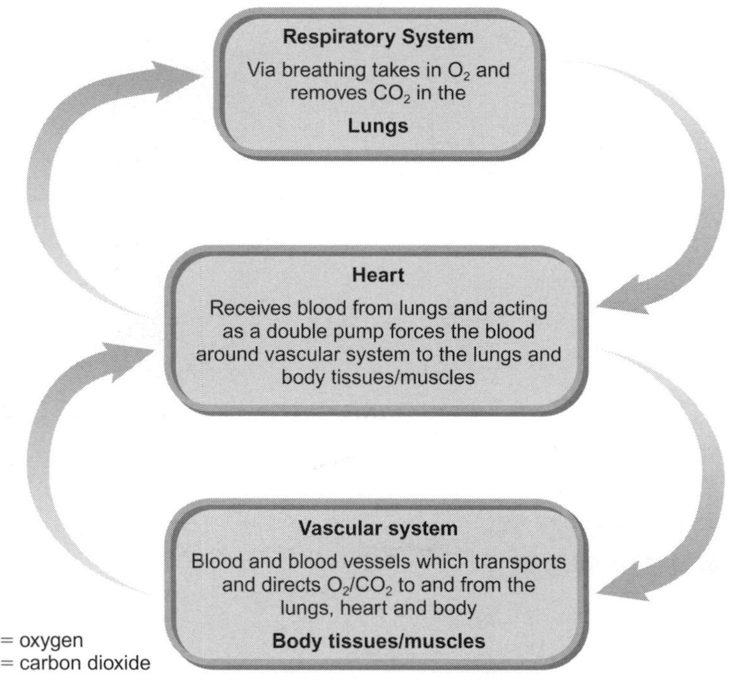

Fig. 4.01 The interaction between the vascular, heart and respiratory system.

Aerobic

Anaerobic

Aerobic is a process taking place in the presence of oxygen. **Anaerobic** is a process taking place in the absence of oxygen.

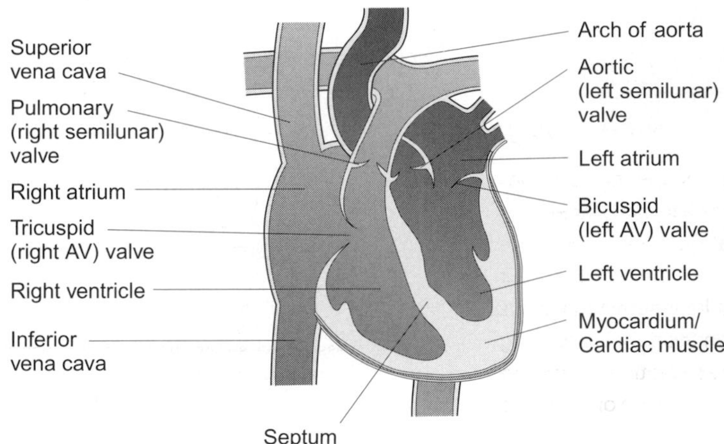

Fig. 4.02 The internal and external structures of the heart.

2 Heart's conduction system linked to the cardiac cycle

Deoxygenated

Oxygenated

The heart acts as a dual-pump action – two separate pumps that work simultaneously to pump blood to two different destinations. The right side pumps **deoxygenated** blood (blood depleted of oxygen) towards the lungs and the left side pumps **oxygenated** blood (blood saturated/loaded with oxygen) towards the rest of the body.

You will be required to link the conduction system to events of the cardiac cycle.

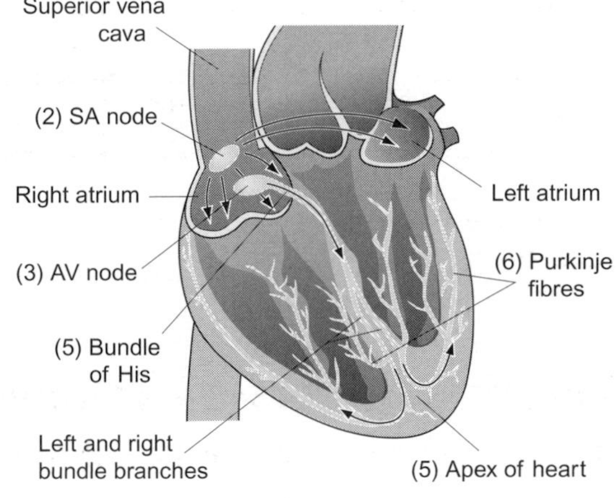

1 The heart is myogenic – it generates/controls its own electrical impulse called the cardiac impulse.
2 Cardiac impulse initiated from SA node (pacemaker) in right atrium.
3 Impulse passes through right and left atrium walls to AV node.
4 Causing both atria to contract, termed 'atrial systole'.
5 AV node conducts impulse down through bundle of his and down through the septum to apex of heart.
6 Impulse travels up around ventricle walls via purkinje fibres.
7 Causing both ventricles to contract, termed 'ventricular systole'.
8 Cycle continues. SA node initiates the next cardiac impulse.

Fig. 4.03 Structures involved in the conduction of the cardiac impulse.

NEED TO KNOW MORE?

For further information on the heart conduction system, see pp. 56–8 in *Advanced PE for OCR, AS*.

The cardiac cycle

The cardiac cycle represents the mechanical events of one heartbeat. One complete cycle lasts approximately 0.8 seconds.

If you are answering questions on the cardiac cycle, remember that the events during the cardiac cycle occur simultaneously. What takes place on the right is occurring at the same time on the left side of the heart.

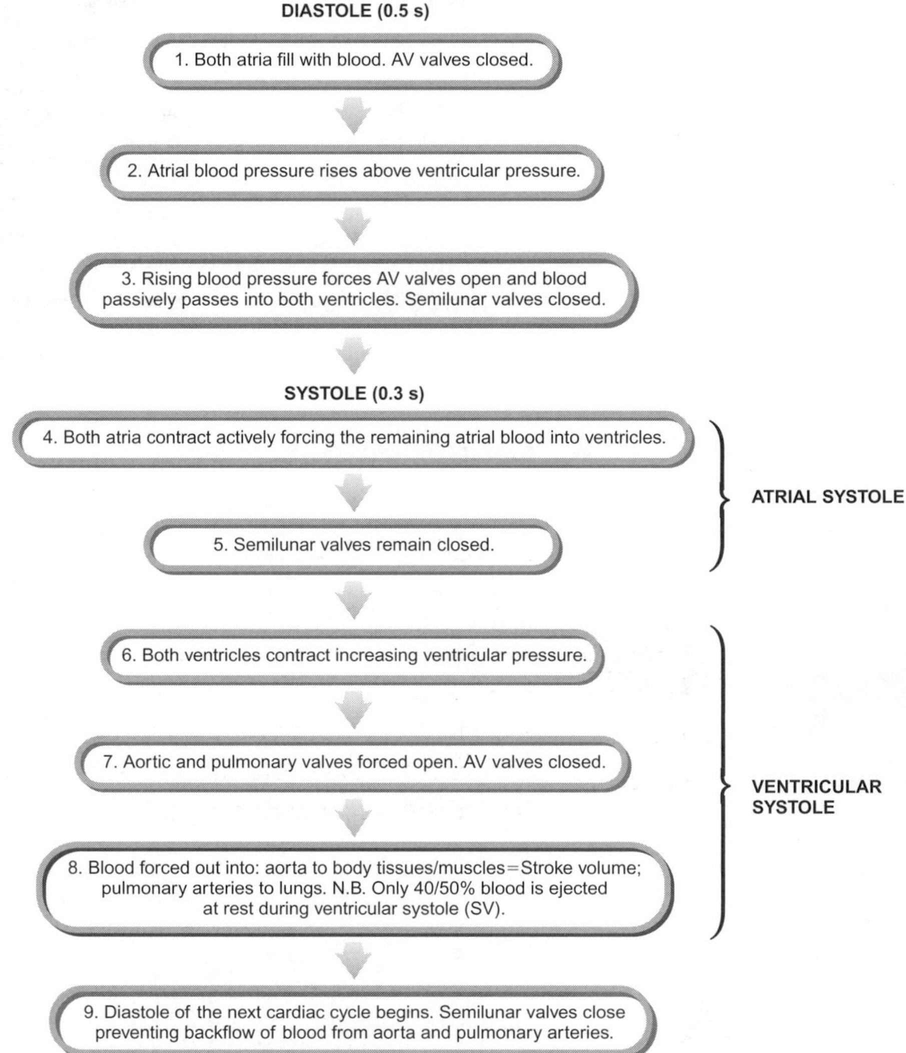

Fig. 4.04 Summary diagram of the phases and sequence of events occurring during the cardiac cycle.

3 Resting heart rate – volumes and definition

Heart rate

Bradycardia

Hypertrophy

The **heart rate** represents the number of times the heart ventricles beat in one minute. The average resting heart rate is 72 beats per minute. The maximal heart rate is: 220 − Age (for example 220 − 17 = 203).

Bradycardia is a resting heart rate that is below 60 beats per minute. It may indicate a high level of aerobic fitness. It may also be due to **hypertrophy,** which is an increase in size of the heart muscle wall.

Stroke volume

Stroke volume

The **stroke volume** (SV) is the volume of blood ejected by heart ventricles per beat or the difference in the volume of blood before and after each ventricle contraction. The average resting stroke volume is approximately 70 ml.

- The end diastolic volume (EDV), *before*, is the volume of blood left in the ventricles at the end of the relaxation/filling stage of the cardiac cycle.
- The end systolic volume (ESV), *after*, is the volume of blood left in the ventricles at the end of the contraction/emptying stage of the cardiac cycle.

To calculate SV: **EDV − ESV = SV**

Remember, 1000 ml = 1 l. When calculating blood volumes, always present figures from 1000 and above in litres if referring to stroke volume and l/min if referring to cardiac output.

Cardiac output

This is the volume of blood ejected by heart ventricles in one minute.

Q	=	SV	×	HR
(Litres per minute	=	millilitres per beat	×	beats per minute)
Average:				
5 l/min	=	70 ml	×	72

4 Heart rate response to exercise

	EXERCISE INTENSITY		
DEF	**Resting**	**Sub-maximal** (Moderate)	**Maximal**
SV	60/80ml 80/110ml	80/100ml untrained 160/200ml trained	100/120ml untrained 160/200ml trained
HR	70/72bpm	Up to 100/130bpm	220 – your age
Q	5L/min	Up to 10L/min	20–40L/min

Fig. 4.05 Summary of HR, Q and SV values related to exercise intensity.

Sub-maximal

Sub-maximal refers to exercise performed at an intensity below an athlete's maximal aerobic capacity, or max VO_2 – hence it represents aerobic work.

Stroke volume: response to exercise

Stroke volume increases from values around 60–80 ml per beat at rest to maximal values of around 120 ml per beat during exercise.

SV increases due to:

KEY WORDS

Venous return

Ventricular contractility

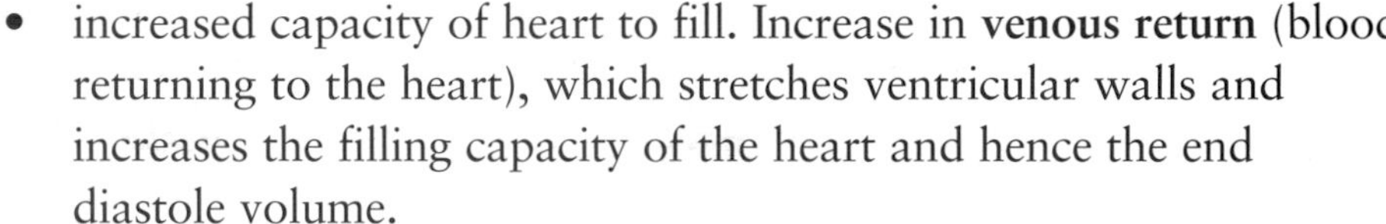

- increased capacity of heart to fill. Increase in **venous return** (blood returning to the heart), which stretches ventricular walls and increases the filling capacity of the heart and hence the end diastole volume.
- increased capacity of heart to empty. A greater EDV provides a greater stretch on the heart walls, which increases the force of ventricular systole (contraction of ventricles). This increases **ventricular contractility** (the capacity of the heart ventricles to contract), which almost completely empties the blood from the ventricles increasing SV.

NEED TO KNOW MORE?

For further information on heart rate and response to exercise, see pp. 61–4 in *Advanced PE for OCR, AS*.

Heart rate: response to exercise

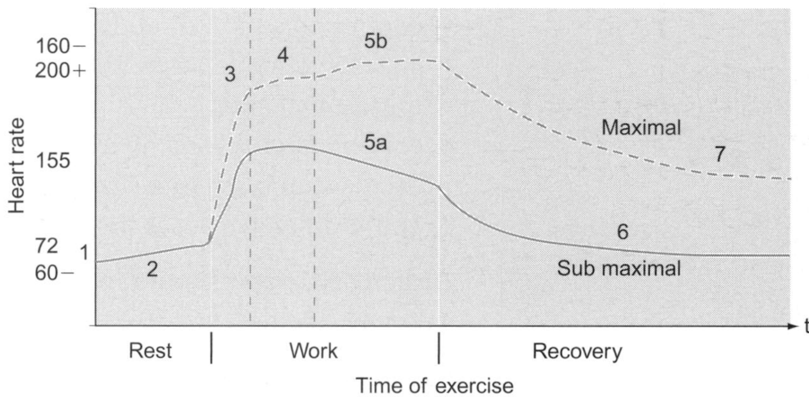

Fig. 4.06 The typical HR response to sub-maximal and maximal work. Stages 1–7 show the significant changes that occur.

1 **Resting heart rate.** The average heart rate is 72, but if a question describes a young, fit aerobic athlete, it may be assumed they will have a resting heart rate below 60, known as bradycardia, due to an increase in stroke volume.

2 **Anticipatory rise.** Heart rate increases even before exercise begins due to the release of adrenalin from adrenal glands, which acts upon the SA node to increase heart rate and ventricle contraction to increase stroke volume (hormonal).

3 **Rapid increase in heart rate** at the start of exercise due to receptors: proprioreceptors (muscle and joint) relating to increased motor activity (neural); chemoreceptors relating to increased CO_2/lactic acid (decreased pH) and decreased O_2 concentrations (neural). Continued/increased effect of adrenalin (hormonal). The receptors stimulate the cardiac centre, which stimulates the SA node to increase heart rate.

4 **Continued but slower increase in heart rate** due to:
- continued effect of chemoreceptors and proprioreceptors (neural)
- increase in blood and heart temperature (intrinsic)
- increase in venous return (blood returning to the heart) (intrinsic).

5A Aerobic sub-maximal work. **Slight fall/steady state plateau** in the heart rate due to:
- oxygen supply equal to the demand of muscles
- baroreceptors slow down heart rate to optimal level to meet O_2 demands via stimulation of parasympathetic vague nerve (neural).

5B Maximal anaerobic work. **Continued rise in heart rate** toward maximal values due to:
- continued action of all factors listed in **2** and **3** above
- anaerobic work where the supply of oxygen is below the muscle demand
- continued anaerobic work increasing lactic acid, which decrease pH, inhibits enzyme action stimulating pain receptors, and ultimately causes muscle fatigue.

A sketched graph should indicate an appropriate maximal HR value by calculating 220 − Age.

6 **Rapid fall in heart rate** as exercise stops due to decrease in stimulation of all the factors in **2**, **3** and **4**.

Oxygen debt

7 **Slower fall in heart rate towards resting values** due to elevated heart rate to help repay **oxygen debt** (additional oxygen consumed during recovery above that usually required when at rest in this time) and remove by-products of respiration, for example, lactic acid. The more intense the exercise, the longer the elevated HR and recovery period due to increase in by-products of respiration that need to be removed.

Cardiac output: response to exercise

Cardiac output, being the product of stroke volume and heart rate ($Q = SV \times HR$), increases directly in line with exercise intensity from resting values of 5 l/min up to maximal values of 40 l/min. See Advanced PE for OCR, AS p. 65.

For further information on heart rate regulation and control, see pp. 64–9 in *Advanced PE for OCR, AS*.

Medulla oblongata

Autonomic

Sensory nerves

Motor nerves

5 Heart rate regulation and control

Cardiac control centre (CCC)

The **medulla oblongata** in the brain contains the cardiac control centre, which is primarily responsible for regulating heart rate.

The CCC is controlled by the **autonomic** nervous system, meaning that it is under involuntary control and consists of **sensory** and **motor nerves** from either the sympathetic or parasympathetic nervous system.

Three main factors affect the activity of the CCC:

- neural control – primary control factor
- hormonal control
- intrinsic control.

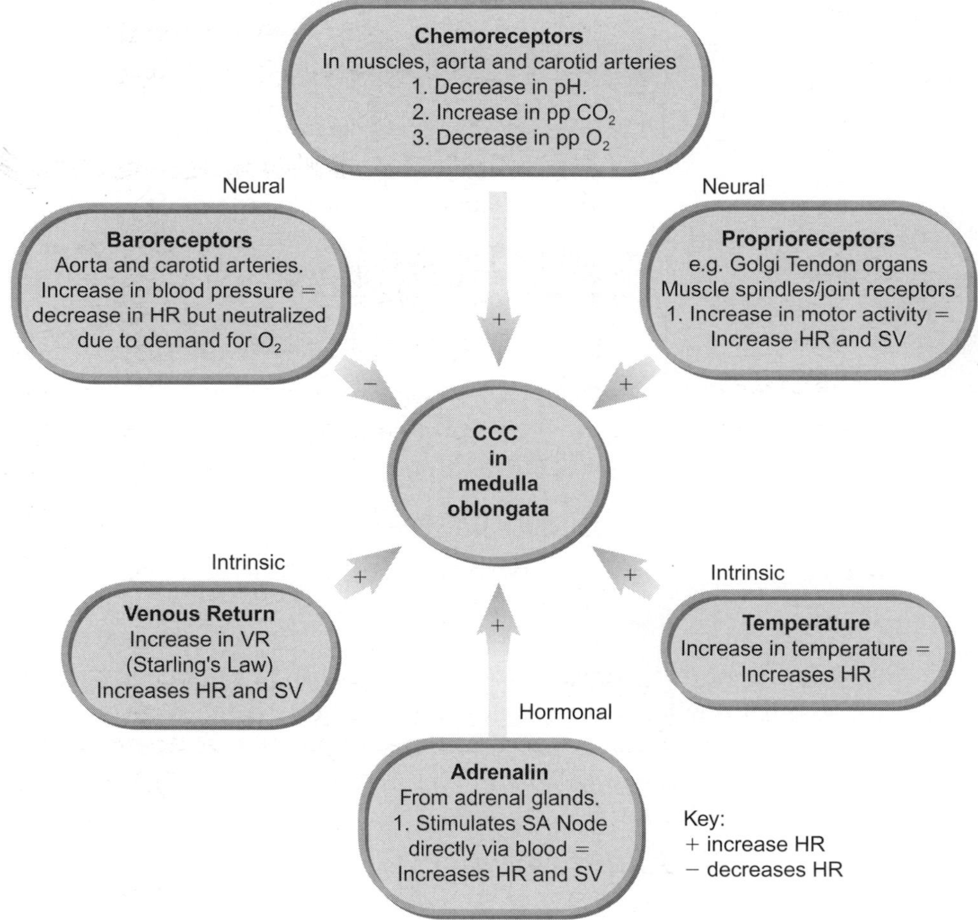

Fig. 4.07 Summary of neural, hormonal and intrinsic factors affecting the activity of the CCC.

The regulation/control of heart rate is best remembered by applying the following points to a flow diagram (fig 4.08).

1 Receptors are sense organs (proprioreceptors, chemoreceptors and baroreceptors) that pick up stimuli/information regarding CO_2, O_2, pH, blood pressure, which is relayed via sensory nerves.
2 Sensory nerves transmit information from receptors to the CCC in the medulla oblongata, which stimulates one of two motor nerves, which stimulate the SA node.
3 **Sympathetic accelerator** nerves increase heart rate.
4 Parasympathetic vagus nerves decrease heart rate.

HOT TIPS

The stimulation of the vagus nerve is decreased simultaneously with the increased stimulation of the accelerator nerve. The effect is a much more rapid increase in heart rate than if just one of the above occurred.

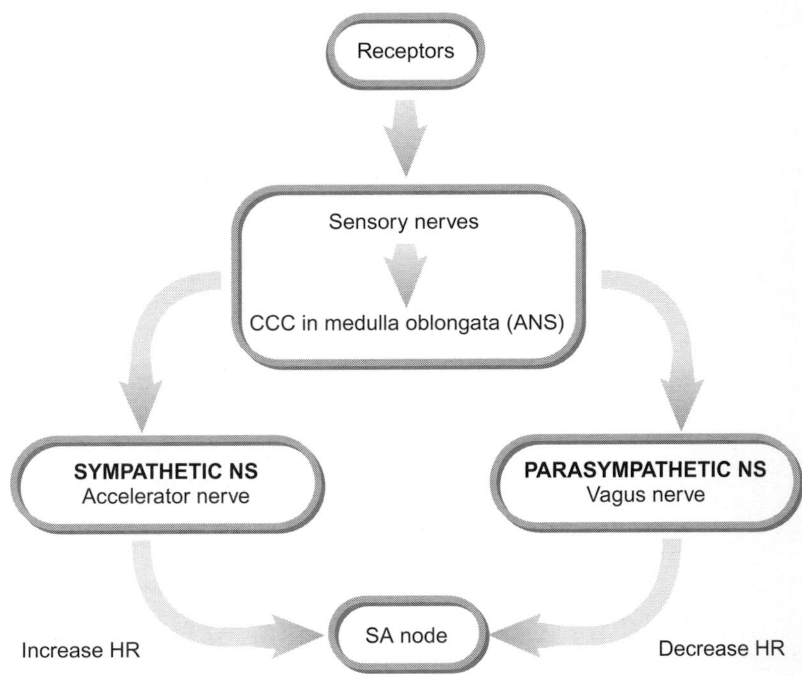

Fig. 4.08 Sympathetic and parasympathetic control of HR via the ANS.

CHECK !

Go back to the overview diagrams on pp. 1 and 21. If you are satisfied with your knowledge and understanding, tick off the sections that you have revised so far. If you are not satisfied, then revisit those sections and refer to the pages in the 'Need to know more?'

Exam practice

1 The measurement of heart rate during training can provide valuable information to the athlete and the teacher/coach.

(a) Sketch a graph onto the plan below to show the heart rate of an athlete who completes a 30-minute aerobic training run.

Show heart rate prior to the training run, during the run and for ten minutes after the run. (4 marks)

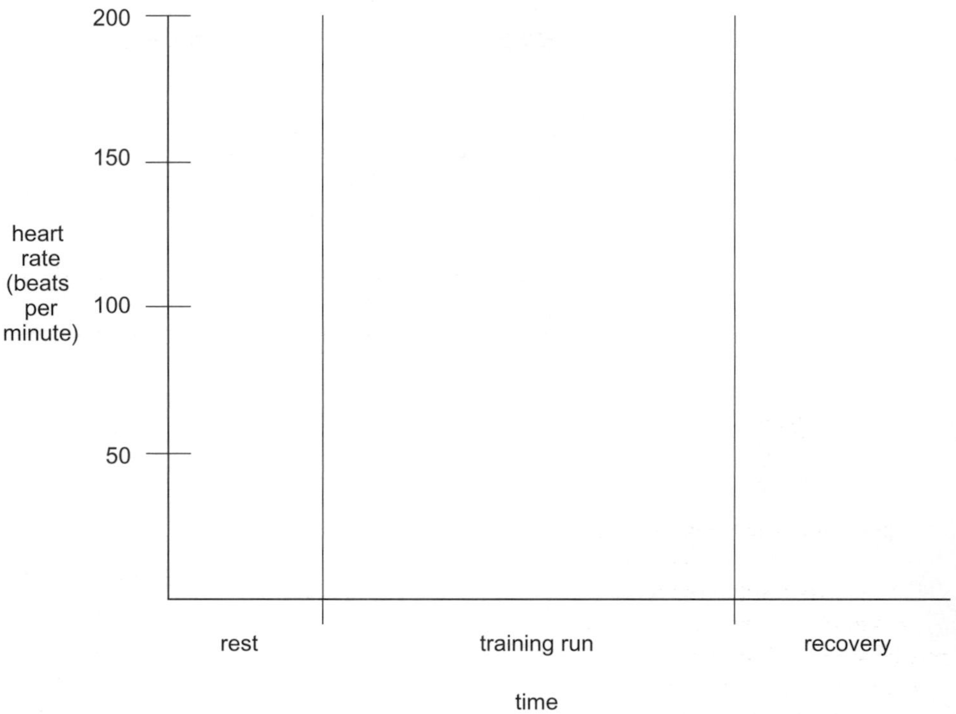

(b) Describe how hormonal control is used to alter heart rate during the training run. (2 marks)

2 During and after exercise, the performer's heart rate will increase and decrease.

(a) Describe how neural control regulates a performer's heart rate. (3 marks)

(b) Endurance (aerobic) performance is dependent upon the heart supplying blood to the muscles. Describe the flow of blood through the heart during the cardiac cycle (diastole and systole). (4 marks)

3 The heart plays an essential role during prolonged exercise.

(a) Define the terms 'heart rate', 'stroke volume' and 'cardiac output'. (3 marks)

(b) Describe how the conduction system of the heart controls the cardiac cycle. (4 marks)

Now go to p. 145 to check your answers.

Chapter 4 Part II: **Control of blood supply**

Chapter overview

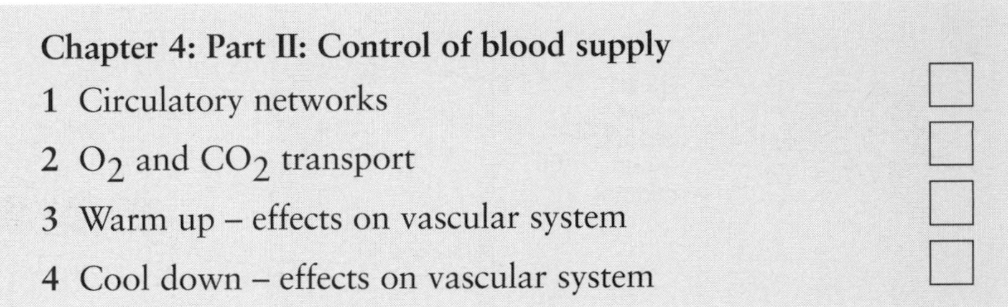

Chapter 4: Part II: Control of blood supply

1 Circulatory networks ☐

2 O_2 and CO_2 transport ☐

3 Warm up – effects on vascular system ☐

4 Cool down – effects on vascular system ☐

For further information on control of blood supply, see pp. 73–84 in *Advanced PE for OCR, AS.*

Tick the box when you are satisfied with your level of knowledge and understanding for each topic within this chapter.

- The vascular system controls blood supply. It consists of blood and blood vessels that transports and directs O_2 and CO_2 to and from the lungs, heart and body tissues/muscles.
- Cardiac output is distributed to the various organs/tissues of the body according to their need/demand for oxygen.
- The blood represents the substance that actually carries/transports the O_2 and CO_2.
- The vast system of blood vessels represents a system of tubing/plumbing that directs and delivers the flow of blood towards the body tissues/muscles.

1 Circulatory networks

Smooth muscle

Vasodilate

Vasoconstrict

Venodilate

Venoconstrict

Blood vessel structure

- All blood vessels have three layers except for single-walled capillaries.
- Arteries and arterioles walls have a large muscular middle layer of involuntary **smooth muscle** to allow them to **vasodilate** (widen) and **vasoconstrict** (narrow) to alter their shape/size to regulate blood flow.
- Arterioles have a ring of smooth muscle surrounding the entry to the capillaries that they control the blood flow into. Called pre-capillary sphincters, they can vasodilate and vasoconstrict to alter their shape/size to regulate blood flow.
- Capillaries have a very thin, one-cell-thick layer to allow gaseous exchange to take place.

- Larger veins have pocket valves to prevent the back flow of blood and direct blood in one direction back to the heart.

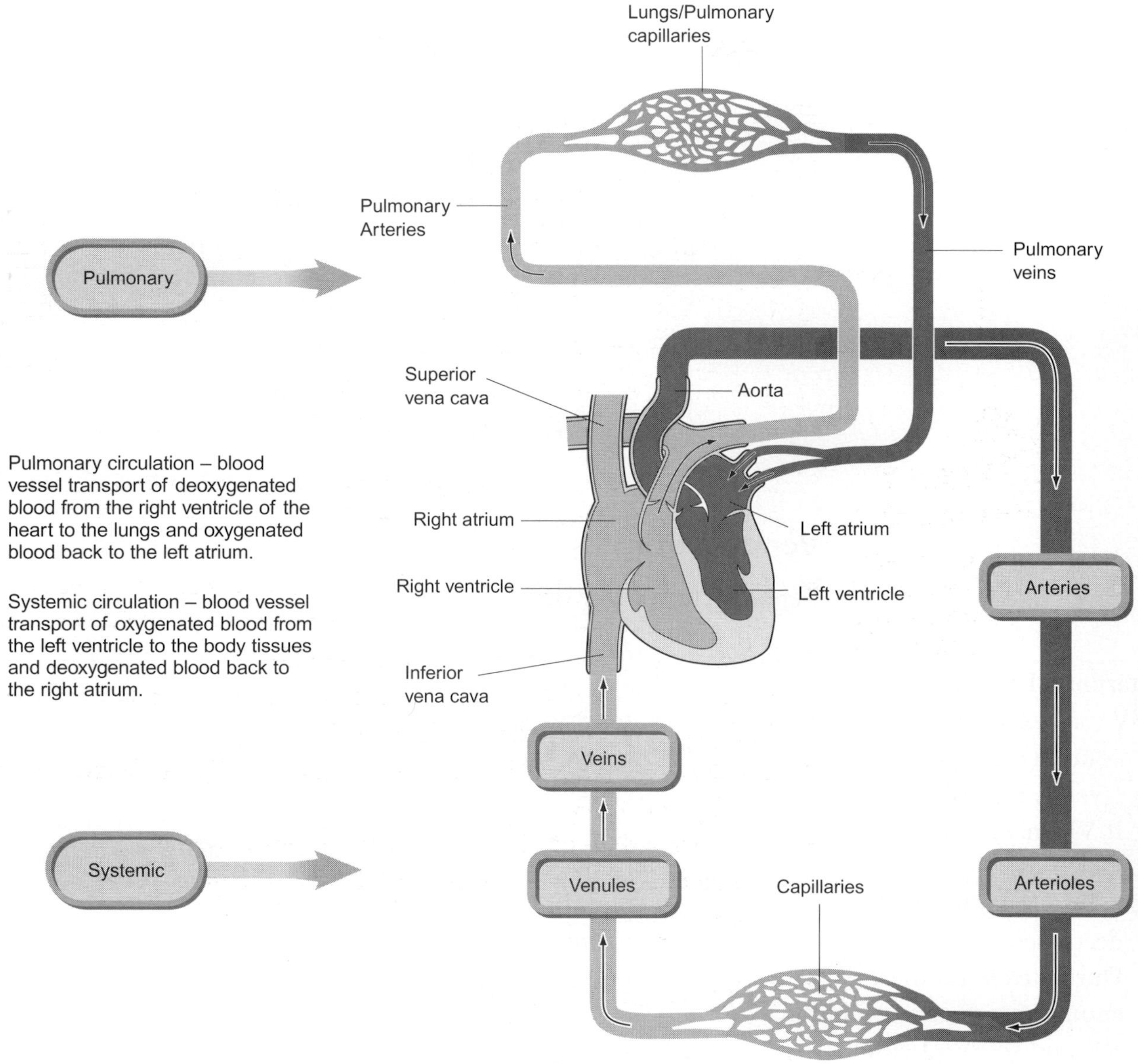

Pulmonary circulation – blood vessel transport of deoxygenated blood from the right ventricle of the heart to the lungs and oxygenated blood back to the left atrium.

Systemic circulation – blood vessel transport of oxygenated blood from the left ventricle to the body tissues and deoxygenated blood back to the right atrium.

Fig. 4.09 Blood vessels of the systemic and pulmonary circulation.

HOT TIPS

Remember that pulmonary arteries and veins **do not** carry blood normally associated with arteries and veins. Exam questions often use the location of either the pulmonary artery or vein as a starting/reference point to test your knowledge of heart structure.

- Venules and veins have a much thinner muscular layer, allowing them to **venodilate** (widen) and **venoconstrict** (narrow) to a lesser extent, and a thicker outer layer to help support the blood that sits within each valve.

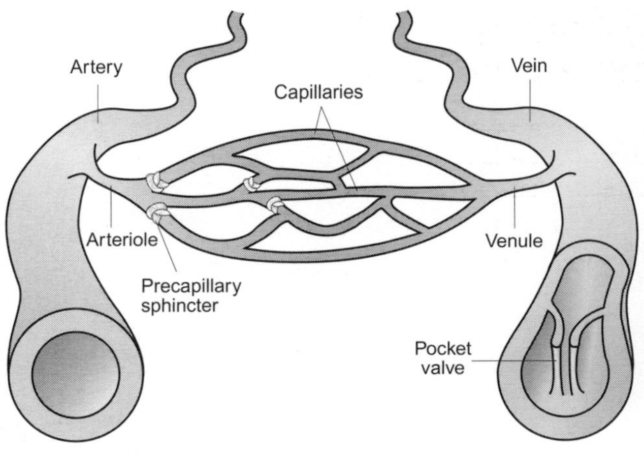

Fig. 4.10 Comparison of common structure of arteries, capillaries and veins.

Venous return

Venous return is the deoxygenated blood returning to the heart.

Starling's Law of the heart
'SV (Stroke volume)/Q (cardiac output) is dependent on VR (venus return)'

- If VR increases, SV/Q increases.
- If VR decreases, SV/Q decreases.
- During exercise there is not enough pressure to maintain VR and so SV/Q would decrease.

Blood pooling

- Insufficient pressure to push blood back towards the heart causes blood pooling (blood sits in pocket valves of veins).
- Active cool down prevents blood pooling after exercise by maintaining the muscle and respiratory pumps.

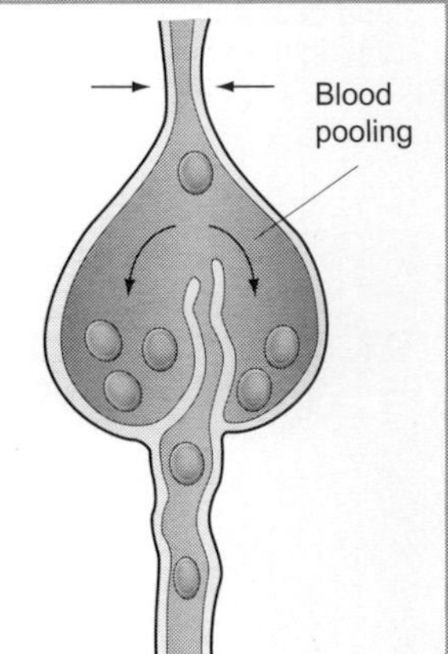

Venous return mechanism's
Five mechanisms help maintain VR during exercise:

1 pocket valves
2 skeletal muscle pump
3 respiratory pump
4 smooth muscle
5 gravity.

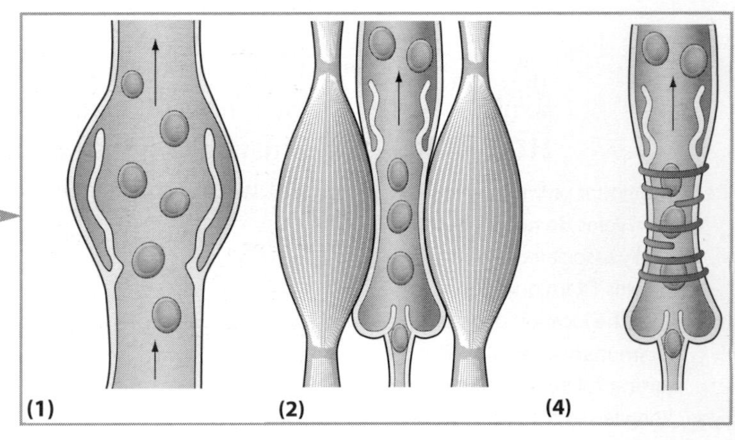

For further information on redistribution of cardiac output between organs and muscles during exercise, see pp. 79–81 in *Advanced PE for OCR, AS*.

Distribution of cardiac output at rest and during exercise

At rest

- Only fifteen to twenty per cent of resting cardiac output is supplied to the muscles.
- The remaining cardiac output (80–85 per cent) supplies the body's organs, for example kidneys, liver, stomach, and intestines.

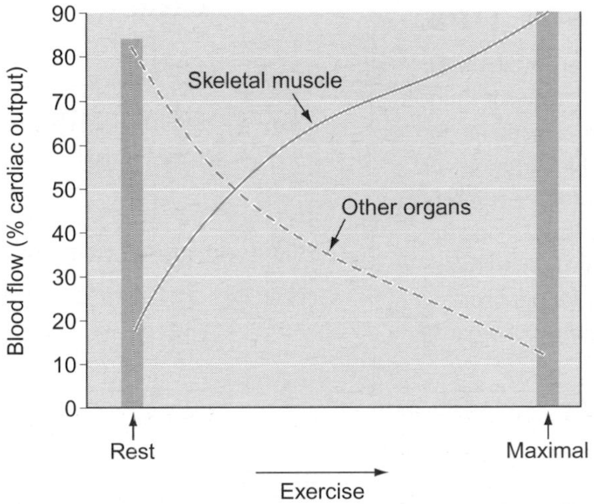

Fig. 4.11 Redistribution of cardiac output between organs and muscles during exercise.

During exercise

- Increased cardiac output (80–85 per cent) is supplied to the working muscles as exercise intensity increases.
- Decreasing percentage of cardiac output is supplied to the body's organs.
- Blood supply to the brain is maintained.
- Increased blood supply to the skin during lighter work to reduce body temperature, but decreases as exercise intensity increases.
- The process of redistributing cardiac output is called the '**vascular shunt mechanism**'.
- Skeletal muscle arterioles and pre-capillary sphincters vasodilate, increasing blood flow to working muscles.
- Organ's arterioles and pre-capillary sphincters vasoconstrict, decreasing blood flow to organs.

For further information on the vasomotor control centre, see pp. 77–82 in *Advanced PE for OCR, AS.*

Vasomotor control centre

Vasomotor control centre (VCC)

- Located in the medulla oblongata.
- Chemoreceptors and baroreceptors stimulate VCC.
- VCC stimulates the sympathetic nervous system, which controls blood vessel lumen diameter of organs and muscles.
- This controls the vascular shunt mechanism:

Up to 4 marks are available for explaining the vascular shunt mechanism. 2 marks are for vasodilation (1 for arterioles or muscles, 1 for pre-capillary sphincters of muscles); 2 marks are for vasoconstriction (1 for arterioles of organs, 1 for pre-capillary sphincters of organs).

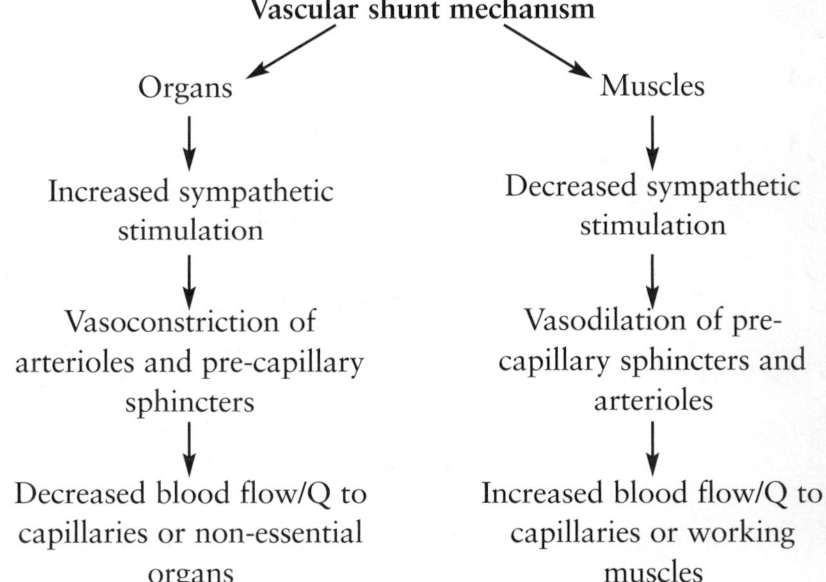

For further information on O_2 and CO_2 transport, see pp. 82–3 in *Advanced PE for OCR, AS.*

2 O_2 and CO_2 transport

O_2 and CO_2 is transported via the blood.

O_2

- 97 per cent transported within the protein haemoglobin, packed with red blood cells, as oxyhaemoglobin (HbO_2).
- 3 per cent within blood plasma.

CO_2

- 70 per cent dissolved in water as carbonic acid.
- 23 per cent carbaminohaemoglobin ($HbCO_2$).
- 7 per cent dissolved in plasma.

3 Warm up – effects on vascular system

- Gradual increase in blood flow/Q due to vascular shunt mechanism, via:

1 Vasoconstriction of arterioles/pre-capillary sphincters to organs decreasing blood flow to organs.
2 Vasodilation of muscle arterioles/pre-capillary sphincters increasing blood flow (O_2) to working muscles.

Enzyme

OBLA

- Increased body/muscle temperature increasing transport of **enzyme** activity required for energy and muscle contraction.
- Increased body/muscle temperature, which decreases blood viscosity, improving blood flow to working muscles, and increases dissociation of O_2 from haemoglobin.
- Decreases **OBLA** (onset of blood lactic acid) due to the onset of anaerobic work without a warm up.

4 Cool down – effects on vascular system

- Keeps metabolic activity elevated, which gradually decreases heart rate and respiration.
- Maintains respiratory/muscle pumps, which;
  - prevents blood pooling in veins,
  - maintains venous return,
  - maintains blood flow (SV and Q) to supply O_2, which,
  - maintains blood pressure.
- Keeps capillaries dilated to flush muscles with oxygenated blood, which,
  - increases the removal of blood and muscle lactic acid and CO_2.

CHECK !

Go back to the overview diagrams on pp. 1 and 30. If you are satisfied with your knowledge and understanding, tick off the sections that you have revised so far. If you are not satisfied, then revisit those sections and refer to the pages in the 'Need to know more?'

Exam practice

1 (a) Draw and label a diagram to show how the two circulatory networks (systemic and pulmonary) transport the blood around the body during a training run. (3 marks)

(b) Describe the mechanisms of venous return that ensure enough blood is returned to the heart during the training run. (2 marks)

2 It is often recommended that a performer cools down following a physical activity.

(a) What effects will a cool down have on the vascular system of the performer? (2 marks)

(b) Why is a warm up beneficial to the vascular system of a swimmer? (2 marks)

(c) Describe how oxygen is transported in the blood. (2 marks)

3 As a result of aerobic exercise, there are changes in the control of blood supply around the working body.

(a) Explain why a good venous return is beneficial to performance. (2 marks)

(b) Explain how carbon dioxide is transported in the blood and why this affects performance during physical activities. (4 marks)

(c) Give two mechanisms by which a large percentage of cardiac output is distributed to the working muscles during exercise. Explain why this distribution occurs. (3 marks)

Now go to p. 147 to check your answers.

Chapter 5 **Respiratory system**

Chapter overview

For further information on the respiratory system, see pp. 85–107 in *Advanced PE for OCR, AS.*

Tick the box when you are satisfied with your level of knowledge and understanding for each topic within this chapter.

1 Review of respiratory structures

There are three main respiratory processes:

1 Pulmonary ventilation – the breathing of air in and out of the lungs.

2 External respiration – exchange of O_2 and CO_2 between the lungs and blood.

3 Internal respiration – exchange of O_2 and CO_2 between the blood and muscle tissues.

For further information on the review of respiratory structures, see pp. 86–7 in *Advanced PE for OCR, AS.*

Route of air into the lungs

Nasal/oral cavity
Pharynx
Larynx
Trachea
Left and right bronchii
Bronchiole
Alveoli duct
Alveoli sac
Aveolus
Nasal cavity
Oral cavity
Trachea
Left and right bronchii
Pharynx
Larynx
Bronchiole
Lung
Alveoli duct
Alveoli sac
Pulmonary capillaries
Alveolus
Capillary network on surface of alveolus

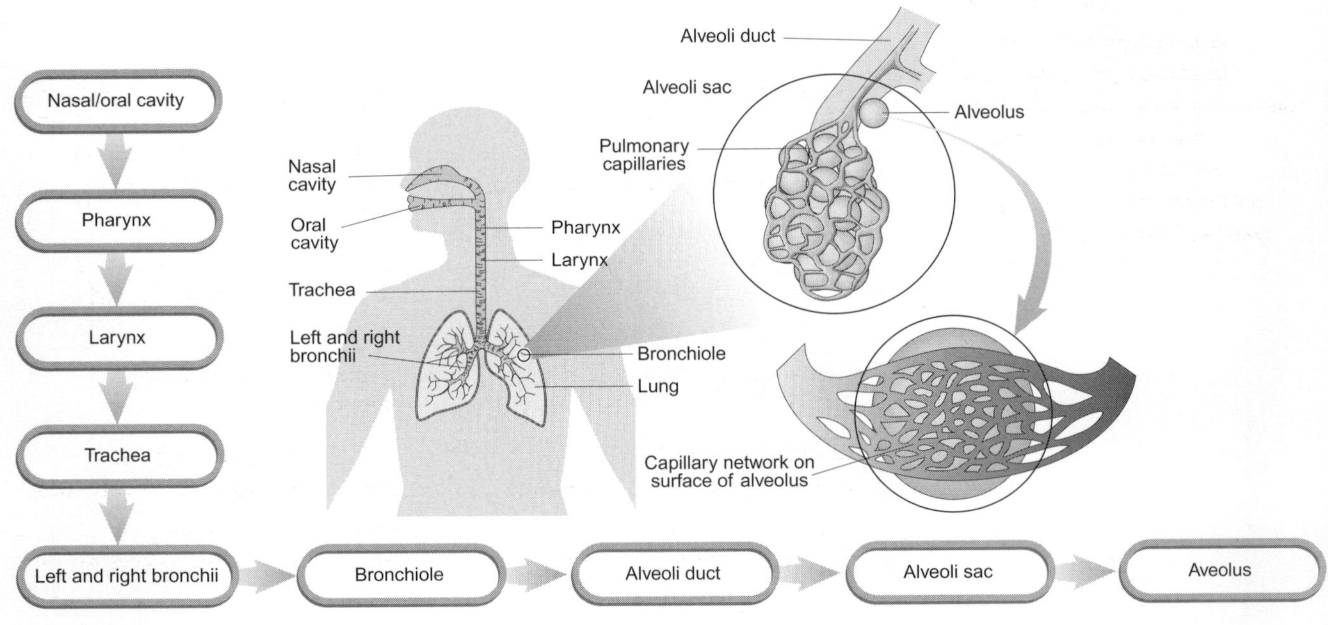

Fig. 5.01 Route of air through the respiratory structure.

Alveoli structure linked to efficiency of gaseous exchange

Good pulmonary lung ventilation
Large/vast surface area of alveoli
Thin/single cell layer of alveoli and capillary respiratory membranes
Moist lining/water helping dissolve and exchange O_2
Capillary wall
Alveolar wall
Red blood cell
Respiratory membrane
Narrow capillaries bringing rbc close to alveoli
LOW ppO_2
HIGH $ppCO_2$
Diffusion of O_2
HIGH ppO_2
Diffusion of CO_2
LOW $ppCO_2$
Red blood cell in capillary
Vast network alveoli capillaries surrounding alveoli
Short diffusion path
Steep diffusion gradients

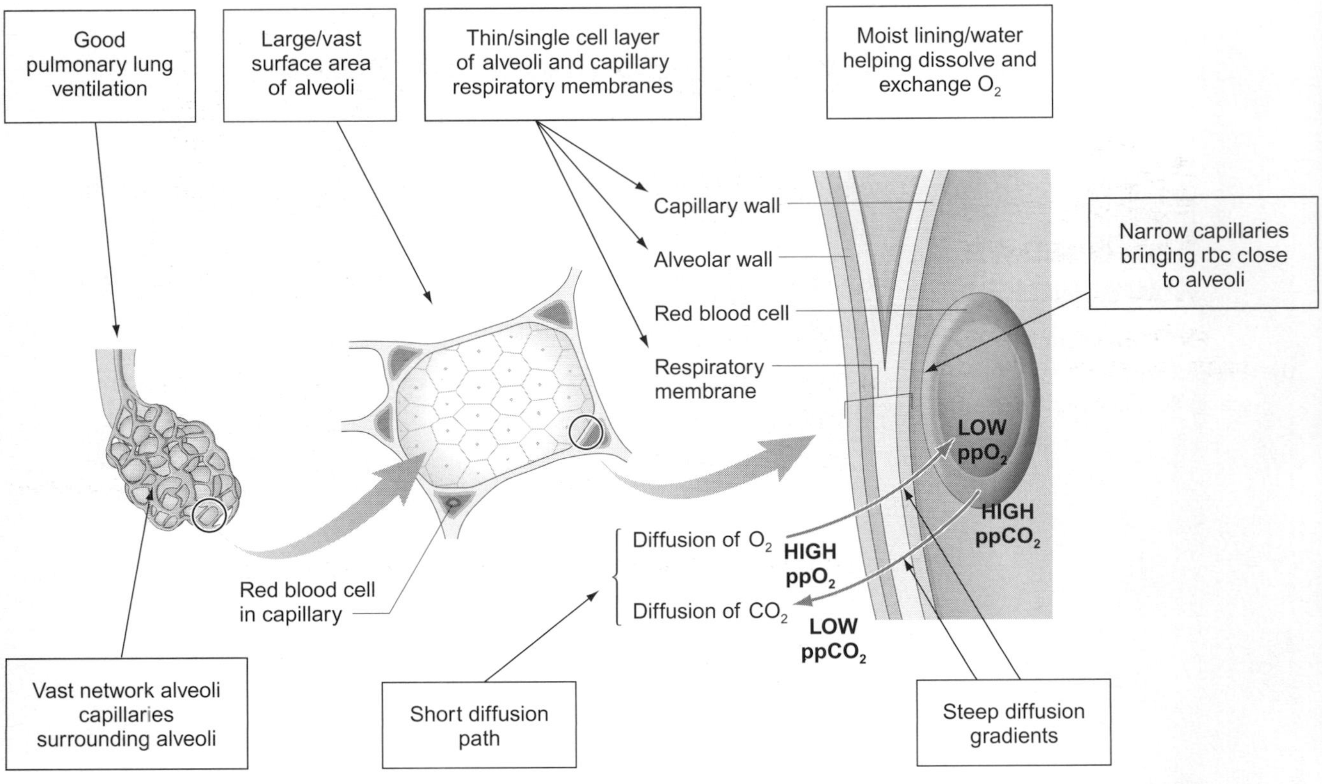

Fig. 5.02 How alveoli structures increase the efficiency of gaseous exchange in the lungs.

HOT TIPS

Respiratory muscles initiate breathing by increasing and decreasing the volume of the lung cavity and therefore lung pressures. Do not make the mistake of thinking the lungs or pressure differences themselves initiate breathing.

2 Respiration at rest

Muscles apply the force to initiate the mechanics of respiration.

(a) Inspiration	(b) Expiration
1 Diaphragm contracts – active External intercostals contract – active	1 Diaphragm relaxes – passive External intercostals relax – passive
2 Diaphragm flattens/pushed down Ribs/sternum move up and out	2 Diaphragm pushed upward Ribs/sternum move in and down
3 Thoracic cavity volume increases	3 Thoracic cavity volume decreases
4 Lung air pressure decreases below atmospheric air (outside)	4 Lung air pressure increases above atmospheric air (outside)
5 Air rushes into lungs	5 Air rushes out of lungs

NEED TO KNOW MORE?

For further information on respiratory volumes at rest, see pp. 90–2 in *Advanced PE for OCR, AS*.

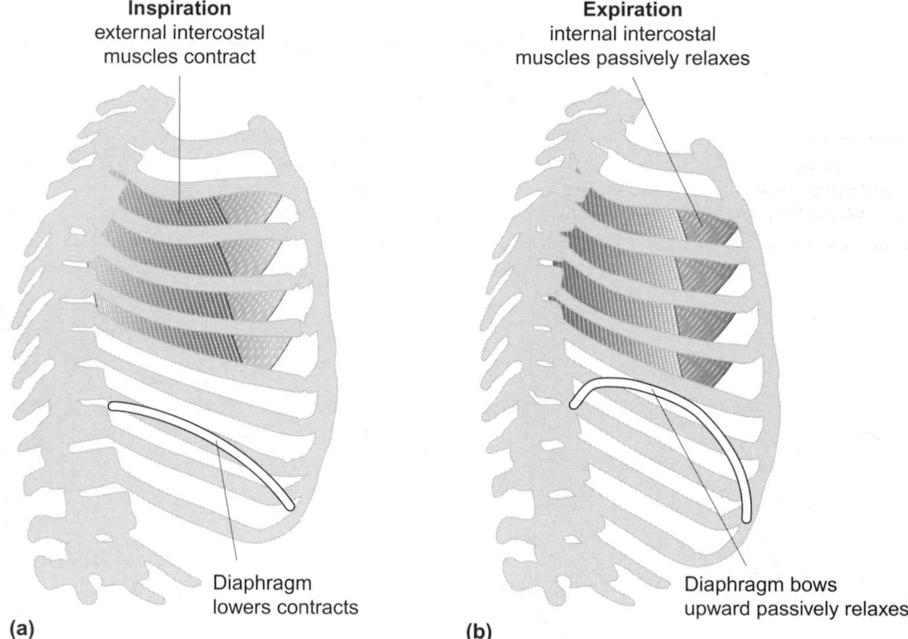

Fig. 5.03 Active inspiration (a) and passive expiration (b) at rest.

Remember the close similarity between these heart and respiratory equations. Do not confuse them when answering heart/respiratory volume questions.

Remember, 'respiratory' refers to air and 'heart' refers to blood.

3 Respiratory volumes at rest

Lung volumes and capacities help calculate the efficiency of the respiratory system by comparing resting with exercising levels.

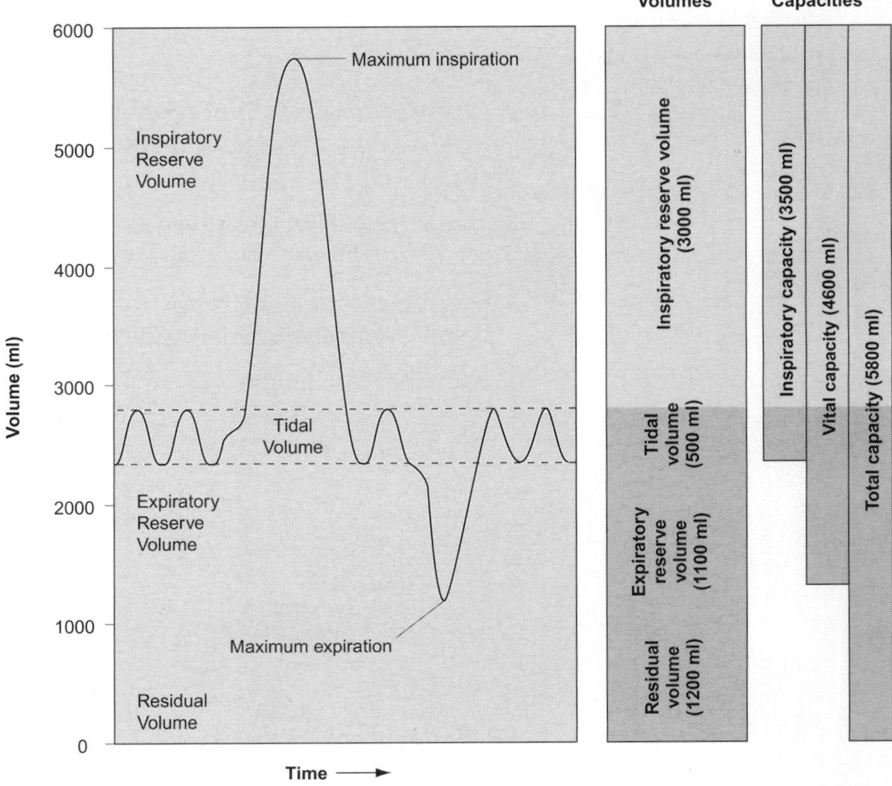

Fig. 5.04 Graph representing a spirometer trace to show respiratory volumes.

Minute ventilation = tidal volume x frequency

VE	=	TV	x	F
	=	500	x	15
	=	7500 ml/min		
	=	7.51 l/min		

Lung volume	Definition	Resting volume
Tidal volume X	Volume of air inhaled/exhaled per breath during rest	500ml per breath
Frequency	Number of breaths in one minute	12–15
= VE Minute ventilation	Volume of air inspired/expired in one minute	6–7.5L/min
Inspiratory reserve volume	Volume of air that can be forcefully inspired after normal TV inspiration	3100ml
Expiratory reserve volume	Volume of air that can be forcefully exhaled after normal resting TV expiration	1200ml
Vital capacity	Maximal volume of air that can be expired after maximal inspiration: VC = TV + IRV + ERV	4800ml
Residual volume	Volume of air remaining in the lungs after a forced expiration	1200ml
Total lung capacity	Maximal volume of air contained in the lungs after a maximal inspiration: TLC = TV + IRV + ERV + RV	6000ml

4 Gaseous exchange

- Gaseous exchange is the exchange of O_2 and CO_2 by the process of diffusion.
- Diffusion is the movement of a gas from an area of high pressure to an area of low pressure.
- Partial pressure is the pressure a gas exerts within a mixture of gases.

Myoglobin

Myoglobin is the red pigment in muscles that stores and transports O_2 to mitochondria within muscles.

You will not be required to know actual partial pressures only if the PP is higher and the reason why

The simplest way to remember whether blood has a high or low PP of CO_2 or O_2 is to think back to the terms 'oxygenated' and 'deoxygenated' blood. If the blood is oxygenated, it has a high PP of O_2 and a low PP of CO_2. Deoxygenated blood has the opposite. Similarly, the tissues/muscles and alveoli PP of O_2 and CO_2 are the opposite to that of the PP of blood within the vessels of the vascular system.

External respiration	
Where	Alveolar-capillary membrane, between alveoli air and blood in alveolar capillaries
Movement	O_2 in alveoli diffuses to blood; CO_2 in blood diffuses to alveoli
Why	PP of O_2 in alveoli higher than the PP of O_2 in the blood so O_2 diffuses into the blood
Why	PP of CO_2 in the blood is higher than the PP of CO_2 in the alveoli so CO_2 diffuses into the alveoli

Internal respiration	
Where	Tissue-capillary membrane, between the blood in the capillaries and the tissue (muscle) cell walls
Movement	O_2 in blood diffuses into tissue; CO_2 in tissues diffuses into blood
Why	PP of O_2 in blood is higher than the PP of O_2 in the tissue so O_2 diffuses into the Myoglobin within tissues
Why	PP of CO_2 in the tissue is higher than the PP of CO_2 in the blood so CO_2 diffuses into the capillary blood

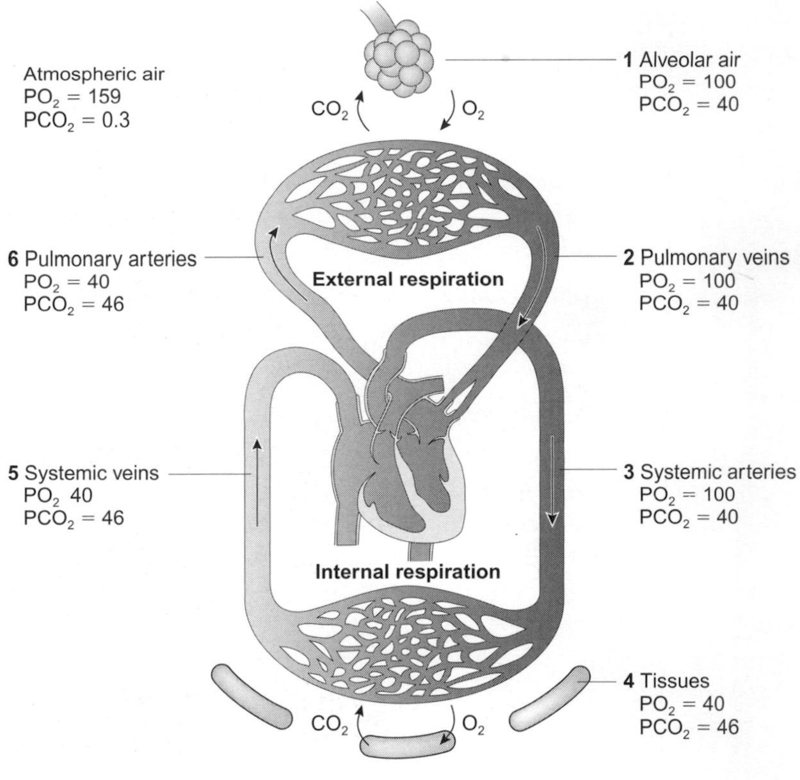

Fig. 5.05 External and internal respiration showing changes in O_2 and CO_2.

5 Respiratory response to exercise

As exercise begins, the demand for O_2 by the working muscles increase and respiration similarly needs to increase.

For further information on respiratory response to exercise, see pp. 94–5 in *Advanced PE for OCR, AS*.

Mechanics of breathing

Additional muscles cause the increase in rate/depth of breathing during exercise.

Inspiration	Expiration
1 Diaphragm contracts External intercostals contract **Sternocleidomastoid** contracts **Scalenes** contract **Pectoralis minor** contracts	1 Diaphragm relaxes External intercostals relax **Internal intercostals** contract (active) **Rectus abdominus/ Obliques** contract (active)
2 Diaphragm flattens with more force Increased lifting of ribs and sternum	2 Diaphragm pushed up harder with more force Ribs/sternum pulled in and down
3 Increased thoracic cavity volume	3 Greater decrease in thoracic cavity volume
4 Lower air pressure in lungs	4 Higher air pressure in lungs
5 More air rushes into lungs	5 More air pushed out of the lungs

6 Lung volume/capacity changes during exercise

As respiration increases in line with exercise, lung volumes and capacities also change during exercise.

Lung volume	Resting volume	Change due to exercise
Tidal volume X	500ml per breath	Increases: up to around 3–4 litres
Frequency	12–15	Increase: 40–60
= VE Minute ventilation	6–7.5L/min	Increase: values up to 120L/min in smaller individuals and up to 180+L/min in larger aerobic trained athletes
Inspiratory reserve volume	3100ml	Decreases
Expiratory reserve volume	1200ml	Slightly decreases
Vital capacity	4800ml	Slight decrease
Residual volume	1200ml	Slight increase
Total lung capacity	6000ml	Slight decrease

Ventilatory response to light, moderate and heavy exercise

Like heart rate, pulmonary ventilation (VE) changes in response from sub-maximal to maximal exercise.

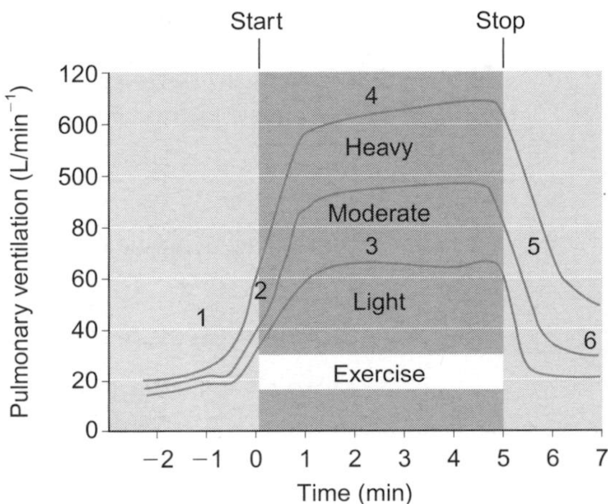

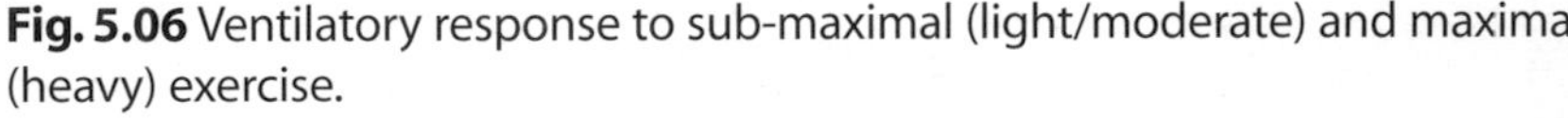
Fig. 5.06 Ventilatory response to sub-maximal (light/moderate) and maximal (heavy) exercise.

HOT TIPS

You will be required to describe and explain the changes in VE from resting to sub-maximal and maximal workloads.

1 **Anticipatory rise** prior to exercise in all three work intensities due to release of hormones and adrenalin, which stimulate the respiratory control centre (RCC).

2 **Rapid rise in VE** at the start of exercise due to neural stimulation of RCC by muscle/joint proprioreceptors.

3 **Slower increase/plateau** in sub-maximal exercise due to continued stimulation of RCC by proprioreceptors, but with additional stimulation from temperature and chemoreceptors (increase in temperature, CO_2 and lactic acid levels and a decrease in blood O_2). Plateau represents a steady state where the demands for oxygen by the muscles are being met by oxygen supply.

4 **Continued but slower increase** in heart rate towards maximal values during maximal work due to continued stimulation from the receptors above and increasing chemoreceptor stimulation due to increasing CO_2 and lactic acid accumulation.

5 **Rapid decrease** in VE in all three intensities once exercise stops due to the cessation of proprioreceptor and decreasing chemoreceptor stimulation.

6 **Slower decrease** towards resting VE values. The more intense the exercise period, the longer the elevated level of respiration required to help remove the increased by-products of exercise – for example, lactic acid.

KEY WORDS

Anticipatory rise

Rapid rise in VE

Slower increase/plateau

Continued but slower increase

Rapid decrease

Slower decrease

NEED TO KNOW MORE?

For further information on ventilatory response to light, moderate and heavy exercise, see pp.96–7 in *Advanced PE for OCR, AS*.

7 Exercise changes to gaseous exchange

An oxygen-haemoglobin dissociation curve informs us of the amount of haemoglobin saturated with O_2.

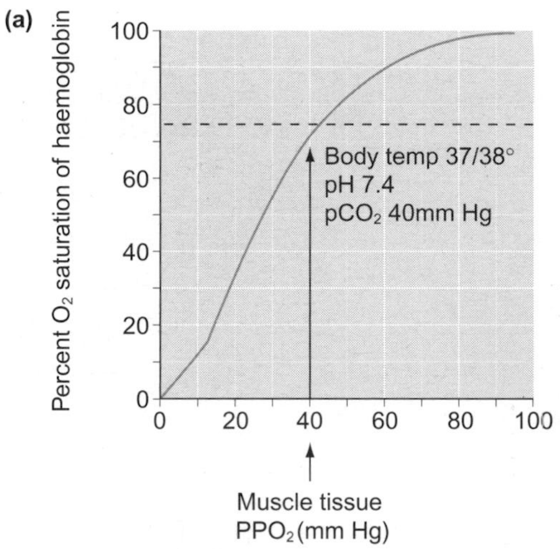

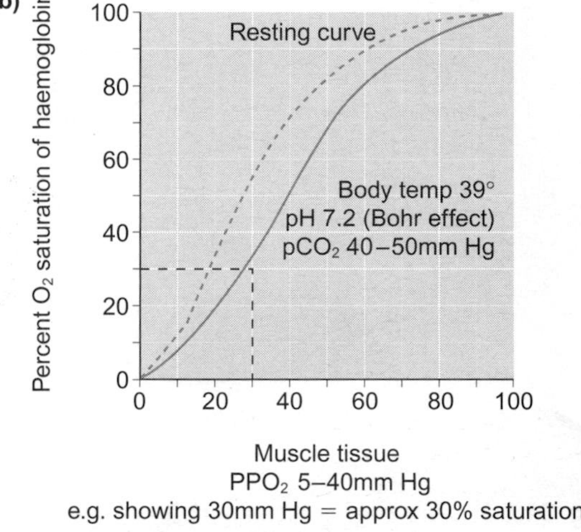

Fig. 5.07 Comparison of oxygen-haemoglobin dissociation curve at rest (a) and exercise conditions (b).

NEED TO KNOW MORE?

For further information on exercise changes to gaseous exchange, see pp. 91–101 in *Advanced PE for OCR, AS*.

Haemoglobin saturation (HbO_2)

During exercise, four factors shift the dissociation curve to the right or, simply put, increase the dissociation of oxygen from Hb in the blood capillaries to the muscle tissue, increasing the supply of O_2 to the working muscles.

1 Increase in PP of CO_2 increasing O_2 diffusion gradient.

2 Decrease in PP of O_2 within muscle increasing O_2 diffusion gradient.

3 Increase in blood and muscle temperature.

4 Bohr effect – increase in acidity (lower pH).

NEED TO KNOW MORE?

For further information on control of breathing, see pp. 101–104 in *Advanced PE for OCR, AS*.

8 Control of breathing

- The respiratory control centre (RCC) is located in the medulla oblongata of the brain and regulates breathing.
- RCC controls breathing via the respiratory muscles.
- The respiratory muscles are under involuntary neural control from the inspiratory and expiratory centres, which stimulate the respiratory muscles at rest and during exercise.
- Figures 5.08 and 5.09 summarize the factors affecting the RCC and respiratory control at rest and during exercise.

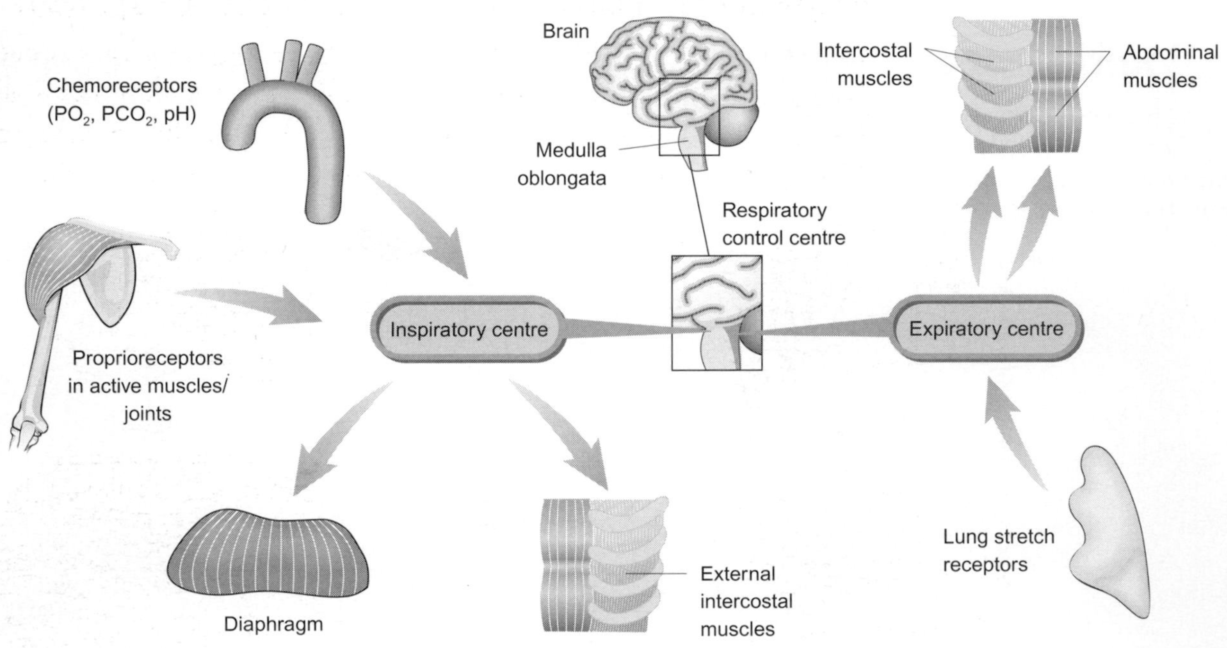

Fig. 5.08 Factors affecting the activity of the inspiratory and expiratory centres in the RCC.

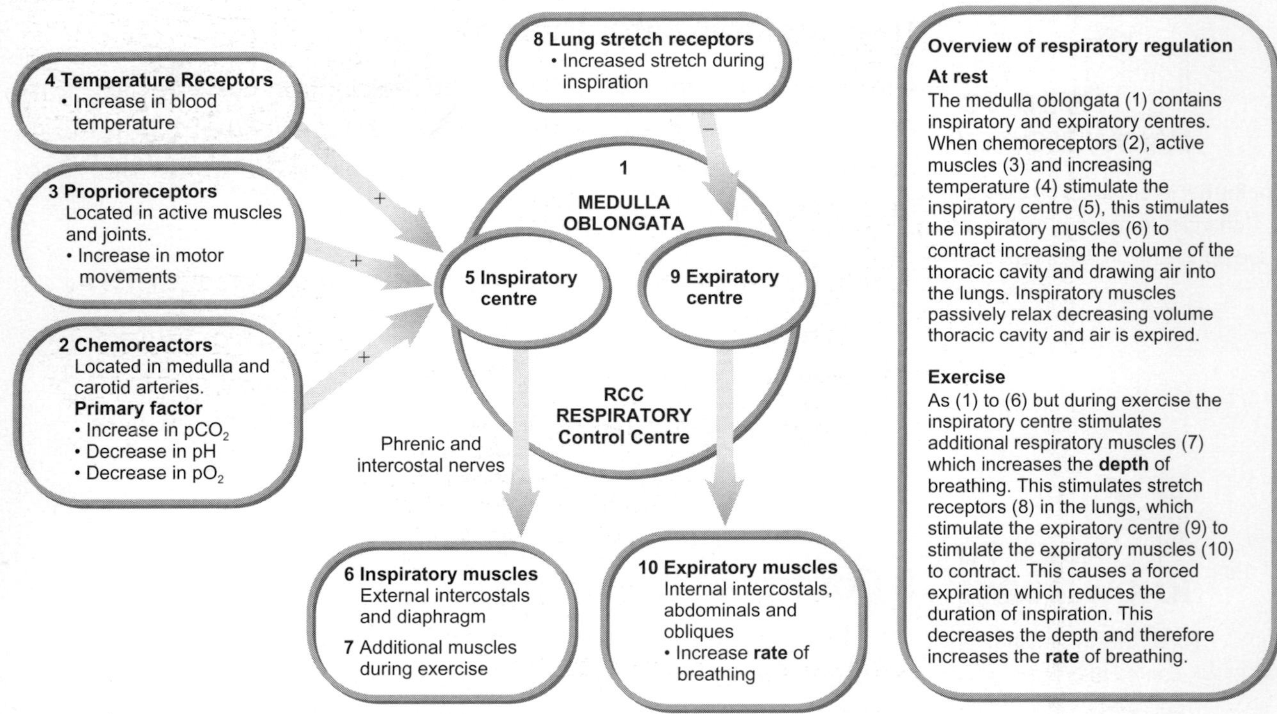

Fig. 5.09 Summary of respiratory control at rest and during exercise.

9 Effects of altitude on the respiratory system

Exposure to high altitude has a significant effect upon performance. At high altitude (above 1500 metres) the PP of oxygen decreases and this has a series of knock-on effects, which decrease the efficiency of the respiratory processes, these are summarized in Fig 5.10 below.

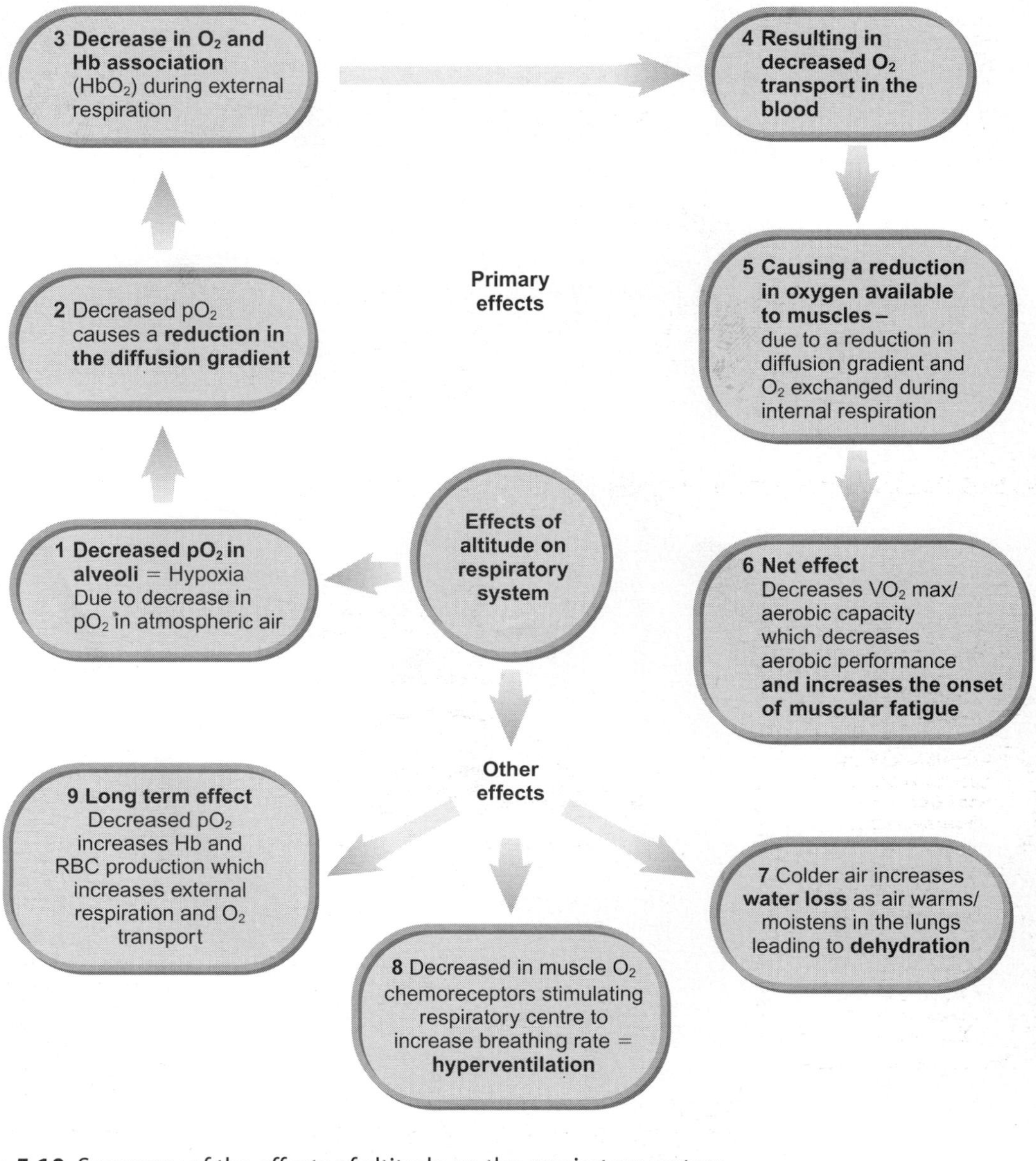

Effects of altitude on respiratory system

Primary effects

1 Decreased pO_2 in alveoli = Hypoxia Due to decrease in pO_2 in atmospheric air

2 Decreased pO_2 causes a **reduction in the diffusion gradient**

3 Decrease in O_2 and Hb association (HbO_2) during external respiration

4 Resulting in decreased O_2 transport in the blood

5 Causing a reduction in oxygen available to muscles – due to a reduction in diffusion gradient and O_2 exchanged during internal respiration

6 Net effect Decreases VO_2 max/ aerobic capacity which decreases aerobic performance **and increases the onset of muscular fatigue**

Other effects

7 Colder air increases **water loss** as air warms/ moistens in the lungs leading to **dehydration**

8 Decreased in muscle O_2 chemoreceptors stimulating respiratory centre to increase breathing rate = **hyperventilation**

9 Long term effect Decreased pO_2 increases Hb and RBC production which increases external respiration and O_2 transport

Fig. 5.10 Summary of the effects of altitude on the respiratory system.

All exam questions on 'control' are incorporated within Figure 5.11. Practise and learn to identify question requirements and which parts of Figure 5.11 to include or leave out.

Cardio-respiratory control

It is easier to learn and understand the control mechanisms of the heart, vascular and respiratory systems as one. Figure 5.11 shows that many of the factors affecting the CCC, VCC and RCC are the same and stimulate the control centres to respond at exactly the same time.

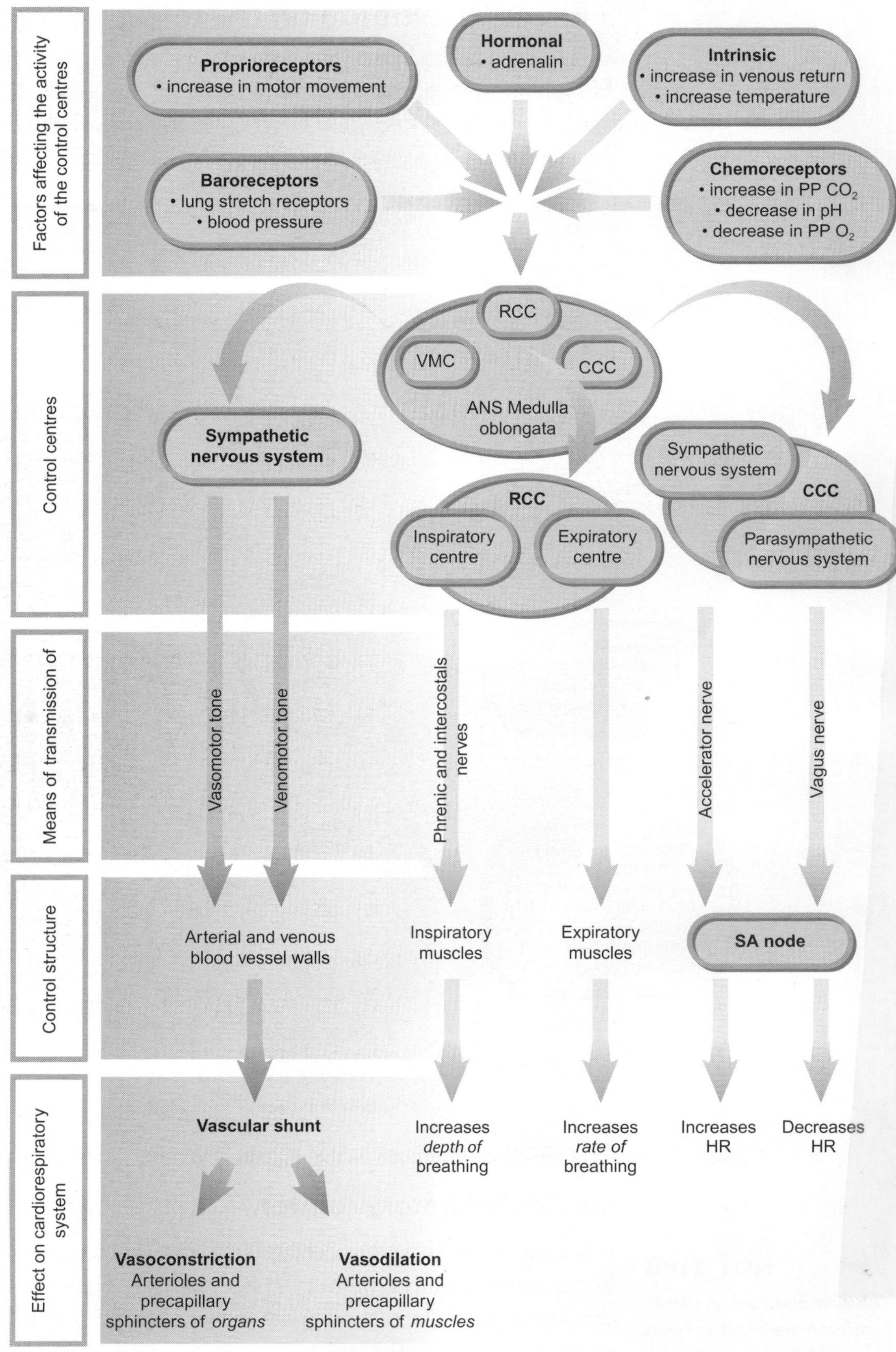

Fig. 5.11 Control and regulation of cardio-respiratory control during exercise.

CHECK !

Go back to the overview diagrams on pp. 1 and 37. If you are satisfied with your knowledge and understanding, tick off the sections that you have revised so far. If you are not satisfied, then revisit those sections and refer to the pages in the 'Need to know more?'

Exam practice

1 The figure below shows a spirometer trace of lung volumes of an athlete at rest.

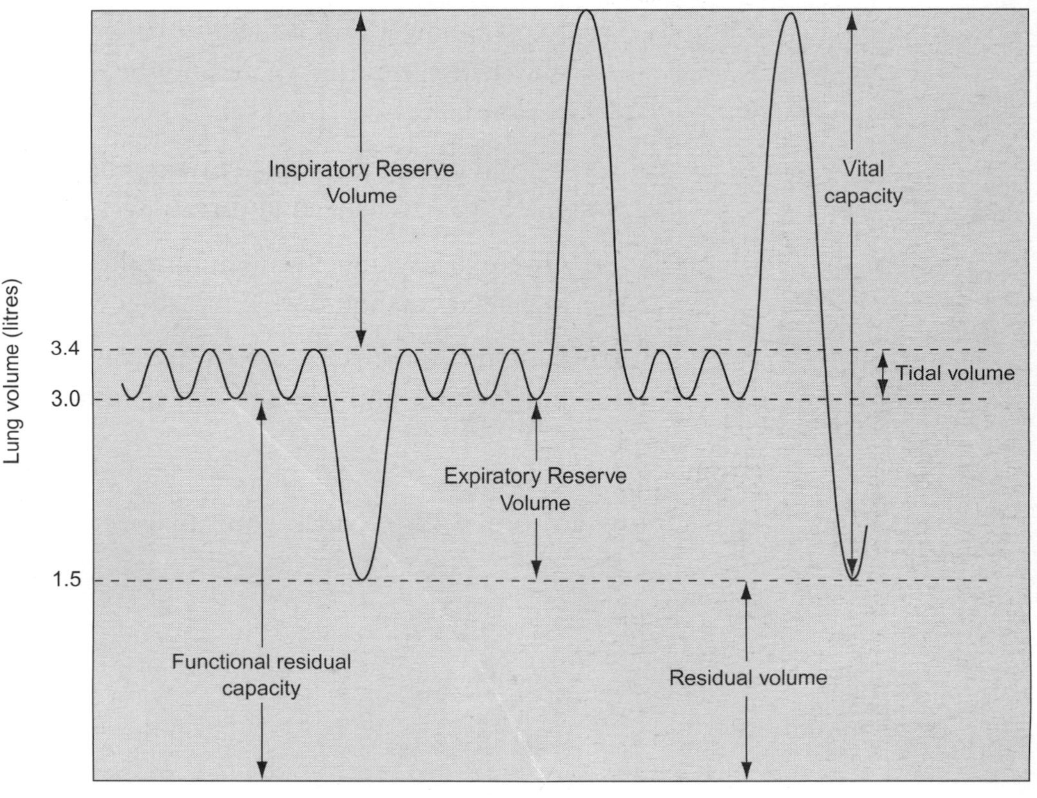

Identify the changes you would expect to see in the following three lung volumes from resting to exercising conditions, for example, during aerobic exercise:

(a) tidal volume

(b) inspiratory reserve volume

(c) expiratory reserve volume. (3 marks)

2 Why would endurance performance decrease when performing at altitude? (2 marks)

3 During prolonged physical activity, the performer needs to take in more oxygen and remove carbon dioxide. Explain how oxygen is exchanged at the alveoli during exercise and why this would be beneficial to performance. (3 marks)

4 Explain how the structure of the lungs enables efficient exchange of gases. (2 marks)

5 During a marathon, the performer must increase the volume of gas exchanged in the lungs and at the muscles.

(a) Describe the changes in the mechanics of breathing during inspiration that allows the performer to exchange larger volumes of gas. (2 marks)

(b) Explain how gas is exchanged between the blood and the muscle tissue during exercise. Why is this beneficial to performance? (3 marks)

6 At rest and during physical activities, the performer varies the volume of gas exchanged in their lungs.

(a) Give typical minute ventilation values for a twenty-year-old fit athlete at rest and during maximal exercise. (2 marks)

(b) Describe how neural control enables the athlete to increase lung volume and why this is beneficial for performance. (3 marks)

Now go to p. 149 to check your answers.

Unit 2: Movement skills

Unit overview

Unit 2: Movement skills

Chapter 6: Defining, developing and classifying skills in PE ☐
Chapter 7: Information processing ☐
Chapter 8: Control of motor skill in PE ☐
Chapter 9: Learning skills in PE ☐

Tick the box when you are satisfied with your level of knowledge and understanding within each chapter.

Chapter 6 **Defining, developing and classifying skills in PE**

Chapter overview

Chapter 6: Defining, developing and classifying skills in PE

1 Developing and classifying skills in PE ☐

2 Application of classification in determining practice types ☐

3 Identifying the differences between skills and abilities ☐

4 Motor skill development ☐

NEED TO KNOW MORE?

For further information on defining, developing and classifying skills in PE, see pp. 108–28 in *Advanced PE for OCR, AS*.

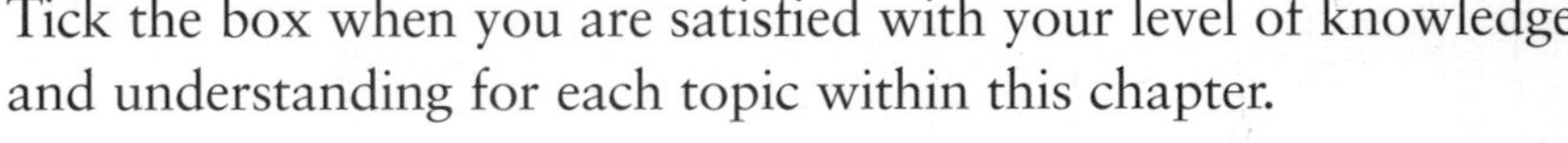

Tick the box when you are satisfied with your level of knowledge and understanding for each topic within this chapter.

1 Developing and classifying skills in PE

Fig. 6.01 Skill as a special task – the Fosbury flop.

HOT TIPS

Learning this definition will help you remember the characteristics of skill; that is,

- learned
- predetermined results (goal directed)
- maximum certainty (consistent)
- minimum outlay of time and energy (efficient).

What is skill?

The term skill can be used in different ways – as:

- a descriptive word: for example, how consistent, successful and technically correct a performer is
- a specific act: for example, a badminton serve
- a series of movements with a clearly defined objective: for example, volleyball.

KEY WORDS

Cognitive skill

Perceptual skill

Motor skill

Perceptual/psychomotor skills

Knapp's definition of skill states that 'skill is the learned ability to bring about predetermined results with maximum certainty, often with the minimum outlay of time or energy or both'.

For further information on the characteristics of skill, see pp. 109–10 in *Advanced PE for OCR, AS.*

Make sure that you know the characteristics of skill and can apply them to a practical example.

Characteristics of skill

Characteristic	Practical example
Efficient	Swimmer is able to go through the water with a streamlined body position, fluent stroke, minimum effort, quickly, with a good technique and no great splashes of water.
Consistent	The volleyball player gets their serve in the court nearly every time they serve.
Fluent	The gymnast is able to link the movements of their sequence together without stopping. One movement flows into the next.
Aesthetic	The trampolinist performs good movements that flow together and are very pleasing to look at.
Learned	The tennis serve has been practised over a period of time and can be performed correctly almost every time it is attempted.
Goal directed	The performer knows what they are setting out to achieve. The basketball player knows what type of pass they are attempting to perform and which team mate they are passing to.
Follows a technical model	We know how good the handstand was by comparing it to the perfect demonstration model and the coaching points.

Types of skill

Skill

Cognitive
A skill that involves the mental/intellectual ability of the performer – for example, working out the tactics to use against an opponent who is very good at the net in a game of tennis.

Perceptual
A skill that involves the detection and interpretation of information – for example, who to pass to, where the pass is to go, and how hard to hit the pass in a game of hockey.

Motor
A skill that involves movement and muscular control – for example, swimming lengths of front crawl.

Perceptual/psychomotor
Involves the cognitive, perceptual and motor aspects of skill. They are the most common forms of skill in PE – for example, determining who to pass to, where to pass to, how hard to hit the pass, and actually hitting the pass in a game of hockey.

Make sure that you can explain and give examples of each of these types of skills: cognitive, motor, perceptual and psychomotor perceptual.

Analysing movement skills

We use continua to analyse movement skills. **Continuum** (plural continua) is an imaginary scale between two extremes that shows a gradual increase/decrease in a number of characteristics.

We use continua to classify movement skills because:

- it is difficult to be specific as skills have elements of all characteristics to a greater or lesser extent
- this can change depending on the situation in which they are performed.

There are six continua that you need to be able to use to classify skills:

For further information on types of skills, see pp. 110–11 in *Advanced PE for OCR, AS*.

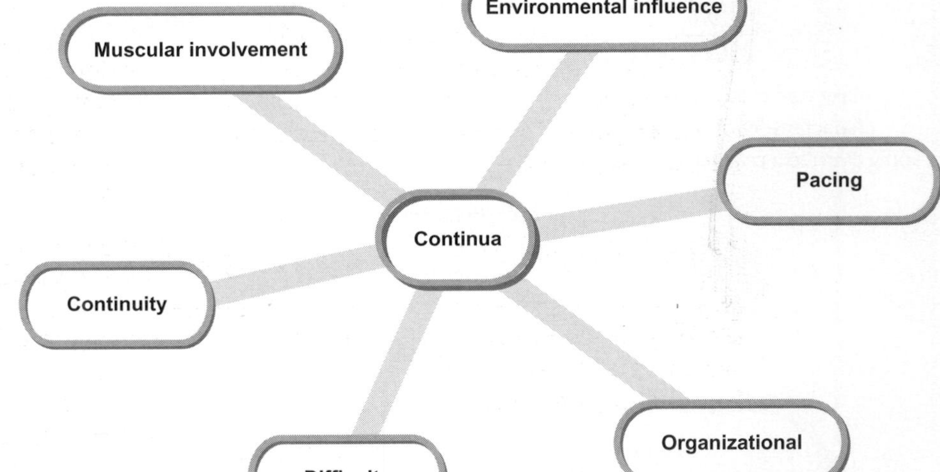

Continuum (plural continua)

Make sure that you can explain why we use continua to classify skills.

Muscular involvement	
Gross ◄	► **Fine**
Involves large muscle movements where there is little concern for precision. For example, hammer throwing is a gross skill.	Involves intricate movements using small muscle groups. Usually involves accuracy and emphasizes hand-eye co-ordination. For example, the wrist and finger action of a spin bowler.

Environmental involvement	
Open ◄	► **Closed**
Movements that are affected by the environment – affected by team mates, opponents, playing surface. Lots of decisions to be made. They are usually externally paced. For example, shooting in basketball/netball.	Not affected by the environment, they are habitual. Follows a technical model. They are usually self-paced. For example, a gymnastic vault.

Continuity		
Discrete ←	**Serial**	→ **Continuous**
Have a clear beginning and end. To be repeated, this single skill must be started again. For example, a penalty in football.	Skills that have a number of discrete elements put together in a definite order to make a movement or sequence. For example, a trampolining sequence.	Have no definite beginning or end. The end of one cycle of the movement is the start of the next. For example, cycling.

Pacing	
Self (internally) paced ←	→ **Externally paced**
The performer is in control and determines when the movement starts and the rate at which it proceeds. For example, a javelin throw.	The control of the movement is not determined by the performer but by the environment (often the opponent). For example, receiving a pass in football or hockey.

Difficulty	
Simple ←	→ **Complex**
Little information to process and few decisions to make. A small number of sub-routines involved where speed and timing are not critical. The use of feedback is not significant. For example, sprinting.	Have a high perceptual load leading to many decisions having to be made. The skill will have many sub-routines where speed and timing are critical, together with the significant use of feedback. For example, a tennis serve.

Organization	
Low ←	→ **High**
Made up of sub-routines that are easily separated and practised by themselves. For example, swimming strokes.	Movement skills where the sub-routines are very closely linked together and are very difficult to separate without disrupting the skill. For example, the golf swing.

HOT TIPS

Whenever you are asked to classify a skill, you also need to be able to explain or justify how you have arrived at your decision. This is because the skill will be different depending on the situation it is performed in. You have to explain the situation the skill is being performed in together with the characteristics it has of the classification you are examining.

Movement skills are usually comprised of several parts that are referred to as sub-routines, for example, breast stroke consists of the following: body position, arm action, leg action and breathing. These sub-routines together make up the movement skill.

2 Application of classification in determining practice types

We classify skills because it tells us:

- how to teach skills
- how we can improve skills
- how we can practise skills.

For further information on application of classification in determining practice types, see pp. 117–20 in *Advanced PE for OCR, AS.*

The conditions in which a skill is learned and practiced should:

- be the same as those in which it is normally performed
- be determined by the nature of the skill
- ensure that **positive transfer** will occur.

Practice conditions are determined by the nature of the skill and in order to establish this several aspects need to be considered. This is called task analysis.

Positive transfer

Using the classification continua will tell us which practice type to use.

Classification	Characteristics	Practice type
Open	High perceptual requirements and decision-making. Unstable changing environment.	Variable practice conditions.
Closed	Stereotyped, habitual movements, stable, fixed environment.	Fixed practice.
Continuous	End of one movement is the beginning of the next, cyclic.	Whole practice.
Discrete	Single integrated action, specific skill, clear end and beginning.	Whole or part dependent on the skill.
Serial	Several integrated actions, several discrete skills put together in a definite order.	Part method, progressive part method.
Low in organization	Skills that can easily be broken into separate parts.	Part method, progressive part method.
High in organization	Skills that cannot easily be broken down into separate parts.	Whole method.
High in complexity	Intricate, highly perceptual with many decisions to be made and many sub-routines to be organized.	Part practice and simplification practices.
Low in complexity	Gross, habitual skills, low perceptual and decision-making aspects, few sub-routines to organize.	Whole method.

Practice types

The different types of practice identified above have the following characteristics

For further information on practice types, see pp. 118–20 in *Advanced PE for OCR, AS.*

Practice type	Characteristics	Example	Advantages
Varied	The practice environment is constantly changing. Techniques and body shape adapted to suit the environment.	Three versus two offensive basketball drill.	Provides the opportunity to develop decision-making and perceptual skills. Improves positional play, selective attention, detecting warning signals, and makes information processing faster. Helps to develop schema. Practice conditions should be realistic.
Fixed	The environment remains the same, that is, stable. The skill is repeated causing the learner to over-learn or groove the skill. The stereotyped action becomes habitual.	Practising drills for the long jump.	The skills become over-learned and stereotyped actions. The movement action never changes. Programmes form and attention can be directed elsewhere.
Part practice	Working on and perfecting isolated sub-routines. Once all the sub-routines have been perfected, they are put together.	Practising body position, leg action, arm action and breathing of swimming strokes, and then putting them all together.	Reduces the possibility of overload. Reduces complexity. Good for skills where there is a danger element. Good for success/motivation.
Progressive part	Learn part 1 – perform part 1. Learn part 2 – perform parts 1 and 2. Learn part 3 –perform parts 1, 2 and 3. Learn part 4 – perform parts 1, 2, 3 and 4.	Lay up shot in basketball. Triple jump.	Good for skills low in organization. Good for serial skills.
Whole practice	The skill is taught without breaking it down into sub-routines or parts.	Basketball dribble, cartwheel or golf swing.	Good for skills that are highly organized or continuous. Allows the learner to get the flow and timing (kinaesthesis) of the skill. Also saves time. Ideally, all skills should be taught by this method.

continued

Practice type	Characteristics	Example	Advantages
Whole part practice	Learner first tries out whole skill to get the feel of the performance. Coach identifies weak parts of the skill and these are practised in isolation. Once perfected, the whole skill is tried again.	Gymnastic/ trampolining sequence.	Learner gets the feel of the movement, allows time to be spent on weaker elements. Saves time.
Simplification	Tasks high in organization and complexity are made easier.	Short tennis where equipment and area is modifed.	Enables learner to be successful. Can help remove danger element, enables learner to be 'physically and mentally' capable.

For further information on identifying the differences between skills and abilities, see pp. 120–4 in *Advanced PE for OCR, AS*.

3 Identifying the differences between skills and abilities

Skill and ability are two different terms although we sometimes use the term 'ability' when we really mean 'skill'.

Characteristics of abilities

Characteristics of skill	Characteristics of ability	Explanation
Learned	Innate/genetically determined	We are born with abilities, which are determined by the genes we inherit from our parents.
Can be modifed with practise	Is stable and enduring	Abilities tend to remain unchanged but can be affected by our experiences and are developed by maturation.
Depends on several abilities	Underpins/supports many skills	Each skill usually needs several supporting abilities if we are going to be able to learn the skill effectively.
There are infinite number of skills	There are presently about 50 identified abilities	

Make sure that you know the differences between skill and ability as this is sometimes asked as an exam question.

Whilst it is accepted that abilities are stable and enduring, some psychologists argue that they can be modified by our experiences and by maturation. Abilities usually improve up to a certain age and then deteriorate as we get older.

Schmidt says that ability is:

> an inherited, relatively enduring trait that underlies or supports various kinds of motor and cognitive activities or skills. Abilities are thought of as being largely genetically determined.

Gross motor abilities

Perceptual motor abilities

Types of ability

There are two types of abilities that you need to know and be able to give examples of. They are **gross motor abilities** and **perceptual motor abilities.**

Gross motor abilities are also known as physical proficiency abilities. They usually involve movement and are related to physical fitness.

Gross motor ability	Example
Dynamic strength	Exerting muscular force over a period of time, for example, press ups.
Static strength	Maximum strength that can be exerted against an external object.
Explosive strength	Energy used effectively for a short burst of effort. For example, jumping in a rugby lineout.
Stamina	Capacity to sustain maximum effort involving the cardiovascular system. For example, running a marathon.
Extent flexibility	Flexing or stretching the trunk and back muscles. For example, touching your toes.
Dynamic flexibility	Making several flexing movements. For example, high knee lift in sprinting.
Gross body co-ordination	Organization of several parts of the body whilst it is moving. For example, performing on the gymnastics parallel bar.
Gross body equilibrium	Being able to maintain balance by using the internal senses and without using vision. For example, performing a handstand.
Trunk strength	The strength of the abdominal muscles. For example, performing sit-ups.
Eye-hand co-ordination	The precise use of hands. For example, hitting a tennis ball.
Static balance	Being able to balance on a stable surface with no movement. For example, standing on one leg.
Dynamic balance	Being able to balance on a moving surface or when moving. For example, skiing.
Eye-foot co-ordination	The precise use of the feet. For example, kicking a ball.

Fig. 6.02 Explosive strength.

Fig. 6.03 Gross body co-ordination.

Perceptual motor abilities usually involve the processing of information, making decisions and putting these decisions into action. These actions are usually movements.

Perceptual motor ability	Example
Multi-limb co-ordination	Being able to organize the movement of several limbs at the same time. For example, swimming front crawl.
Response orientation	Choosing quickly the position to which an action should be made. For example, forehand drive in tennis.
Reaction time	Being able to respond quickly to a stimulus. For example, sprint start.
Speed of movement	Being able to make gross rapid movements. For example, sprinting.
Manual dexterity	Being able to make rapid arm-hand movements involving objects at speed. For example, catching the ball in cricket.
Rate control	Being able to change the speed and direction of responses accurately. For example, following a continuously moving target on a computer game.
Aiming	Being able to aim accurately at a small object. For example, putting in golf.

Make sure that you can identify the supporting or underpinning abilities necessary for different activities. For example, gymnastics needs strength, co-ordination, balance and flexibility.

What do abilities do?

Abilities underpin or support skills. We need several abilities in order to learn a skill effectively, for example, a handstand – balance, strength, body co-ordination. If we have good levels of these abilities then we should be able to learn to do a handstand and other similar gymnastic activities quickly and be able to do them well.

Fig. 6.04 A performer doing a handstand.

Natural athletes

There is no such thing as a 'natural athlete or games player'. Some people are lucky enough to have good levels of the abilities that are required to be successful in a group of activities, which, because the activities are similar, require the same combination of abilities to underpin or support them. These people will still, even though they have these good levels of the necessary abilities, have to learn to apply and co-ordinate them through practise if they are to be successful.

When we learn a skill, we require different abilities at different stages of our learning.

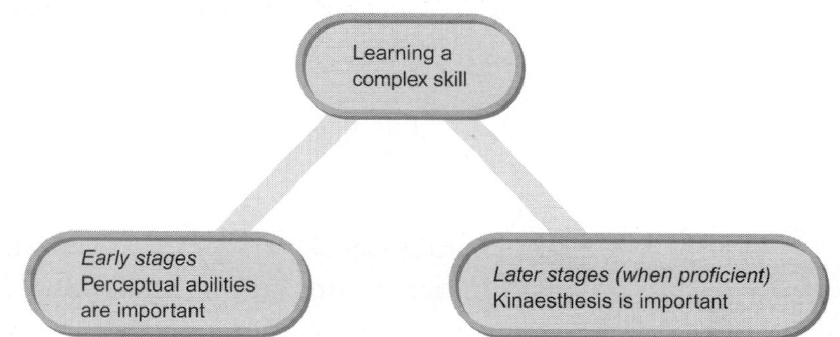

How are abilities developed?

Abilities can be developed during early childhood if:

- children are given a wide range of experiences
- children are given the opportunity to practise
- children receive expert teaching and coaching
- children have access to facilities and equipment
- children have the support of their friends and families who may also be suitable role models.

Examiners sometimes ask how abilities are developed so ensure that you can give examples of each of the points opposite.

For further information on motor skill development, see pp. 125–6 in *Advanced PE for OCR, AS*.

4 Motor skill development

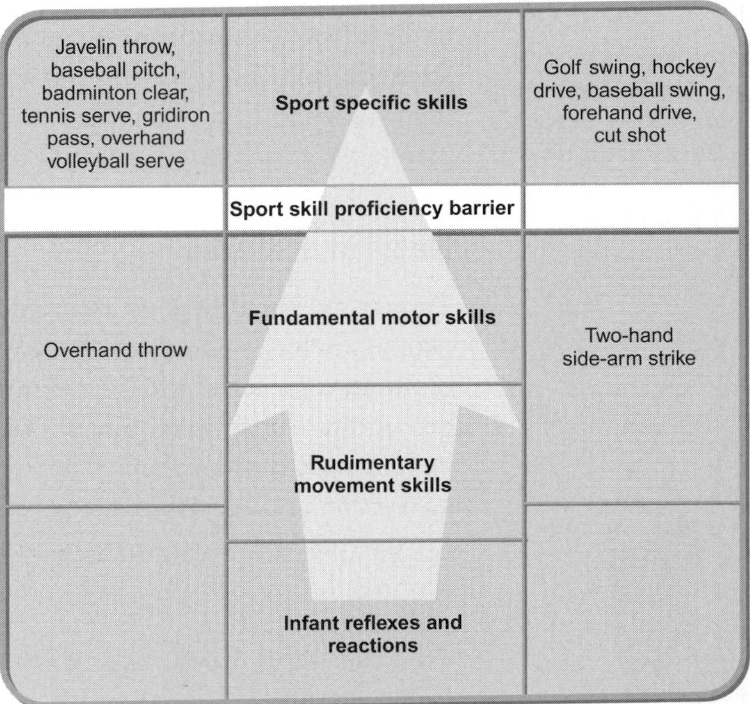

Fig. 6.05 Development stages of skill.

Motor skill development goes through several key stages:

1 Young children use their abilities to learn basic or rudimentary movement skills – for example, walking, running, skipping, pushing, stretching and balancing. These basic movement skills, once mastered, form the basis on which further development will be based.

2 During the early primary school years (four to nine years old), children are physically and mentally capable of learning skills and are also highly motivated and enthusiastic. Expert teaching is needed in order that the child's basic or rudimentary movement skills can be further developed into **fundamental motor skills** (FMS).

Fundamental motor skills

Each FMS has sub-routines against which success can be measured. They have definite coaching points that can be used to ensure that children are learning correctly.

Examples of FMS are:

- catching
- kicking
- running
- dodging
- overarm throwing
- vertical jumping
- two-handed arm strike
- ball bounce
- leap
- forehand strike.

3 Once these FMS have been learned and mastered, they can be developed into sport-specific skills. This is done by adapting and practising each one so that it matches the requirements of the particular sports skill. For example, the FMS of catching, is adapted and practised by children to meet the specific skill requirements of rounders, cricket, netball and rugby. Each of these sport-specific skills have different adaptations in order that the size, shape and hardness of the ball is accounted for. This is the process of developing sport-specific skills from FMS.

Fig. 6.06 The FMS of overarm throwing can be developed into many sport-specific skills.

CHECK !

Go back to the overview diagrams on pp. 51 and 52. If you are satisfied with your knowledge and understanding, tick off the sections that you have revised so far. If you are not satisfied, then revisit those sections and refer to the pages in the 'Need to know more?'

Exam practice

1 A skilful performance in PE could be described as being consistent, efficient and goal directed. Use practical examples to explain each of these three characteristics:

(a) consistent

(b) efficient

(c) goal directed. (3 marks)

2 A sports performer can use both motor and perceptual skills. Use a practical example to explain the term 'perceptual skill'. (2 marks)

3 Use an example from your practical activity experience to describe a self-paced skill and a different example to describe an externally paced skill. (2 marks)

4 Movement skills can be classified by using a continuum. Why is a continuum often used for classifying movement skills? (2 marks)

5 Name a skill from an activity of your choice. Place the skill on each of the continua below and justify its placement.

Name of skill ________________

Environmental influence continuum

Open__________________________________Closed

Justification________________________________ (1 mark)

Continuity continuum

Discrete_________________Serial_____________Continuous

Justification________________________________ (1 mark)

6 The figure below shows the development of motor skills.

Motor abilities ⟶ Motor skills ⟶ Sport-specific skills

Using this figure and a practical example, explain how a named sports-specific skill can be developed. (3 marks)

7 Describe four key characteristics of skilful performance. (4 marks)

8 How would the practice requirements differ for open and closed skills? (2 marks)

Now go to p. 152 to check your answers.

Chapter 7 **Information processing**

Chapter overview

Chapter 7: Information processing

For further information on basic models of information processing, see pp. 129–43 in *Advanced PE for OCR, AS*.

Tick the box when you are satisfied with your level of knowledge and understanding for each topic within this chapter.

1 Basic models of information processing

There are three stages to information processing.

Stimulus

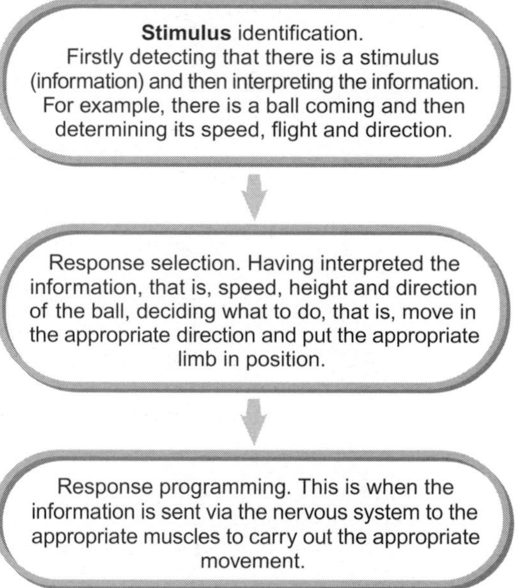

Fig. 7.01 Stages in information processing.

Basic processes of information processing

KEY WORDS

Proprioception

Display

The surroundings/environment the performer is in. For the netball player, this includes ball, team mates, opponents, spectators, umpires and coach/teacher.

↓

Sensory input

Senses detect information, which stimulates their receptors. Senses involved are vision, hearing and **proprioception**. Proprioception is the sense that allows us to know what position our body is in, what our muscles and joints are doing, and to feel things involved in our performance: for example, the ball or hockey stick. It consists of touch, kinaesthesis and equilibrium.

↓

Perception

The process that interprets and makes sense of the information received. It consists of three elements: detection (stimulus is present), comparison (comparing to stimuli in long-term memory), and recognition (matching it to one found in long-term memory).

Perception

Motor programme

↓

Memory

This plays an important role in both the perceptual and decision-making processes. It consists of short-term sensory stores (STSS), short-term memory (STM) and long-term memory (LTM).

↓

Decision making

(translatory mechanism) Once the information has been interpreted, the correct response has to be put into action. This will be in the form of a **motor programme.**

↓

Effector mechanism

The motor programme is put into action by sending impulses via the nervous system to the appropriate muscles to carry out the required actions.

↓

Feedback

Once the motor programme has been put into action, the display changes and new information is created. This new information is known as feedback.

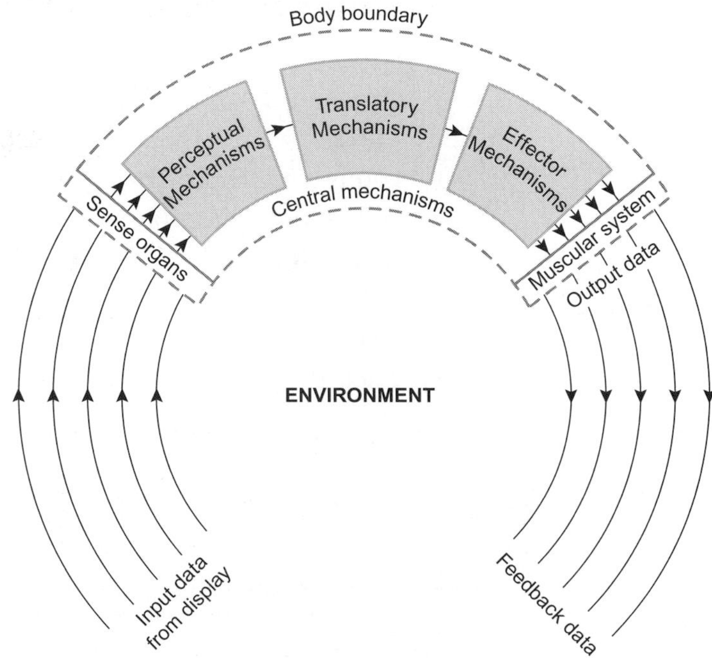

Make sure that you know and understand both Whiting's and Welford's models and are able to draw them and explain their components by the use of practical examples.

Fig. 7.02 Whiting's model for perceptual motor performance.

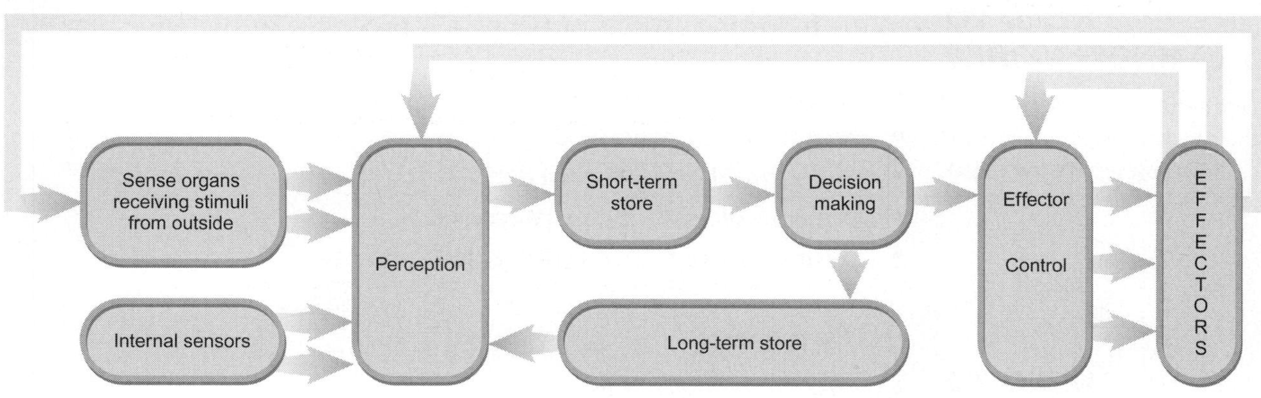

Fig. 7.03 Welford's model of information processing.

Serial and parallel processing

Serial processing of information is processed in stages (sequentially) – for example, a trampolining sequence consisting of:

- jump with 180° turn
- pike straddle jump
- swivel hips
- pike jump
- seat drop
- back drop.

The information would then be processed as follows:

Stage 1	Stage 2	Stage 3	Stage 4	Stage 5	Stage 6
First information for the jump with 180° turn is processed.	Then information for pike straddle jump is processed.	Then information for the swivel hips is processed.	Then information for the pike jump is processed.	Then information for the seat drop is processed.	Then information for the back drop is processed.

For further information on serial and parallel processing, see p. 132 in *Advanced PE for OCR, AS*.

Parallel processing of information is where processes occur at the same time – for example, receiving a pass. The information relating to the following aspects of the pass is processed at the same time:

- speed of ball processed
- height of ball processed
- direction of ball processed
- position of team mates processed
- position of opposition processed.

For further information on memory, see pp. 133–6 in *Advanced PE for OCR, AS*.

2 Memory

Memory is important in:

- interpreting information when it compares information to that of our previous experiences
- determining the motor programme we are going to use to implement the action.

Memory has three components.

1. Short-term sensory stores (STSS)	2. Short-term memory (STM)	3. Long-term memory (LTM)
All information is held for a very short time (0.25–1 second). Capacity is very large. Important information is attended to (selective attention) and that which is not is ignored and will then be lost to be replaced with new information. The perceptual mechanism determines important information (recognition aspect of perception).	Referred to as the 'work place'. Information is compared to that previously learned (comparison aspect of perception). Information is only stored for up to 30 seconds if it is not rehearsed or repeated. It has limited capacity, 7+ or − 2 pieces of information. Capacity can be increased by 'chunking'.	Stores information that has been well learned and practised. Has a very large/infinite capacity. Information is stored for a very long time. Motor programmes are stored in the LTM after much practise. When stored, information is retrieved and compared to new information and found to be the same, this is the recognition aspect of perception.

Strategies to improve retention and retrieval

There are strategies that can be applied to help store and remember information.

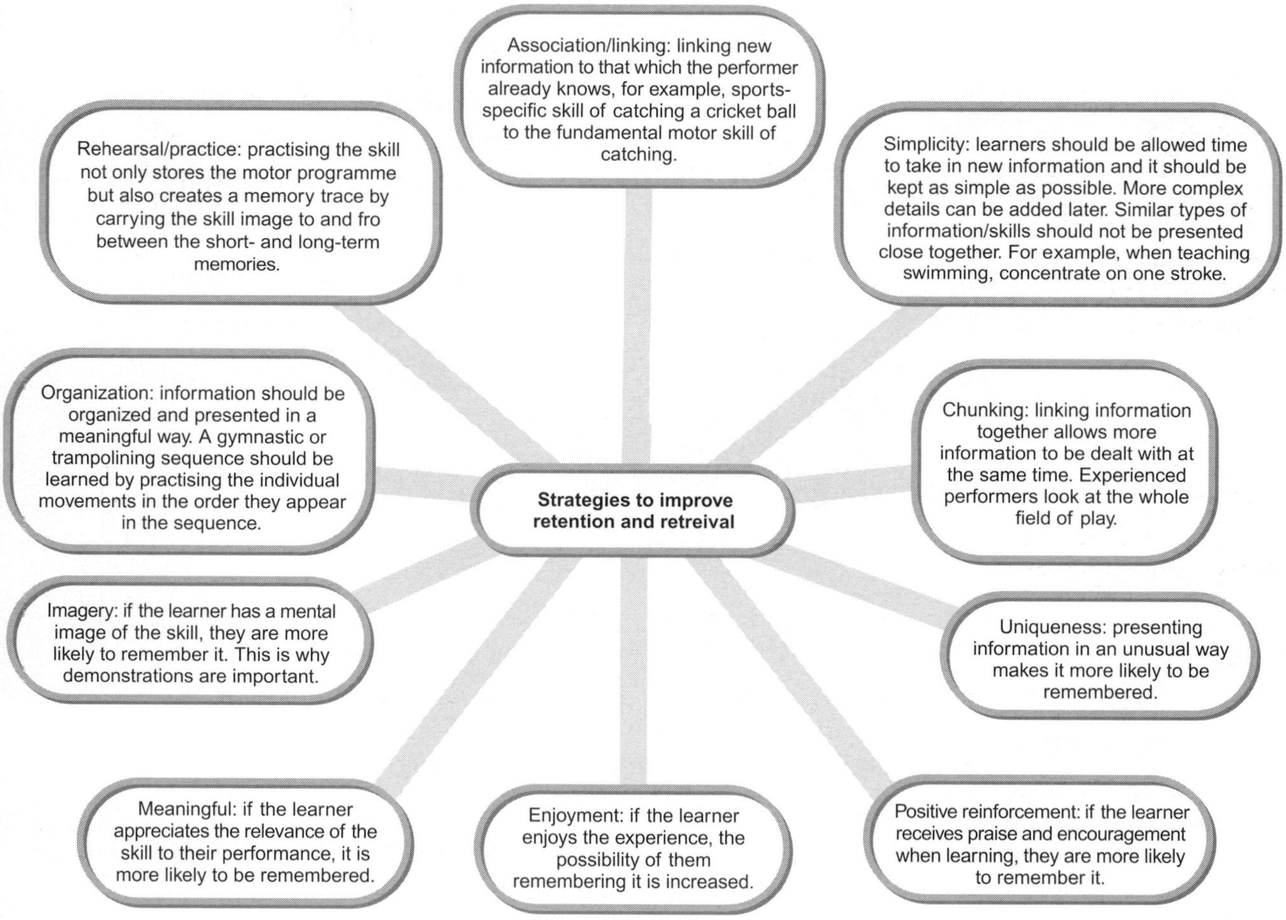

Fig. 7.04 Strategies to improve retention and retrieval.

For further information on reaction time, see pp. 136–40 in *Advanced PE for OCR, AS*.

Reaction time

Movement time

Response time

3 Reaction time

- **Reaction time** – this is the time from the stimulus occurring to the performer starting to move in response to it.
- **Movement time** – this is the time taken from starting the movement to completing it.
- **Response time** – this is the time from the onset of the stimulus to the completion of the movement.

For example, using the 100 metres sprint.

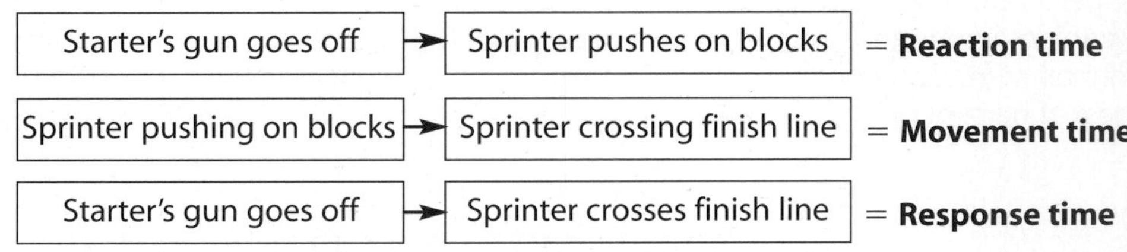

Factors affecting reaction time

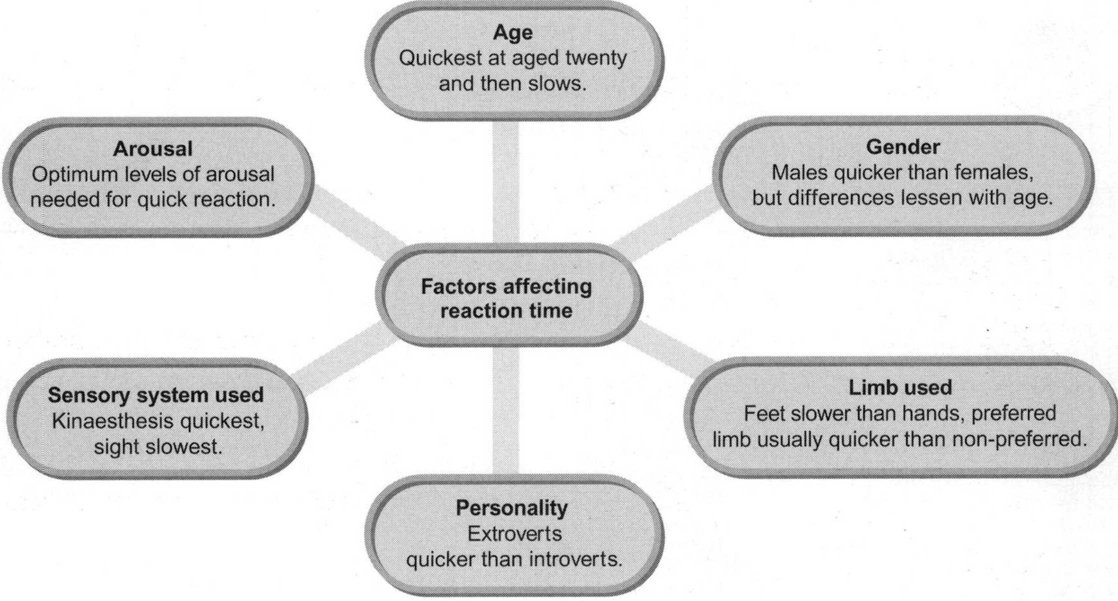

Fig. 7.05 Factors affecting reaction time.

Make sure that you know the definitions of reaction, movement and response times, as well as appreciating the differences between them. Be sure to be able to apply them to a practical activity.

Reaction time can also be affected by external factors.

- If a warning is given, for example, 'set' in sprint start.
- Intensity of stimulus, for example, orange ball for playing football in the snow.
- The likelihood of the stimulus occurring – if the stimulus has a good chance of happening, the reaction will be quicker.

For further information on choice reaction time, see pp. 138–9 in *Advanced PE for OCR, AS.*

Hick's Law

Choice reaction time

Choice reaction time occurs where there is more than one stimulus and/or more than one response. It occurs in many sporting situations.

Hick's Law states that choice reaction time increases linearly as the number of stimulus/choice alternatives increases.

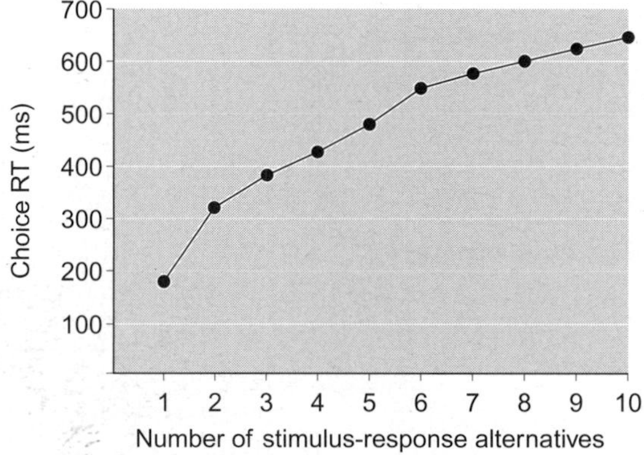

Fig. 7.06 Reaction time increases as the number of stimulus/response alternatives increase.

Hick's Law has important implications in that we should always try to:

- disguise our intentions and therefore increase the number of possible alternatives that our opponents will have to select from. This will increase their reaction time.
- pick up 'cues' as to our opponents intended response in order that this reduces the number of alternatives and therefore reduces our reaction times.

How do teachers/coaches attempt to improve the performer's response time?

Response time can be improved by:

- Practice – the more a stimulus is responded to, the shorter the reaction time becomes, for example, practising sprint starts.
- **Mental rehearsal** – ensures that the performer attends to the correct cues and expects and responds to the correct stimuli. Works on the neuromuscular system. Better for complex tasks with a lot of information processing, for example, passing in hockey.
- Experience – doing the activity enhances the performer's awareness of the probability of the stimulus occurring, for example, practising passing in hockey.
- Stimulus – response compatibility. If the response is the one that you would normally make, it will be quicker, for example, practising marking for set plays in a team game.
- Warm up – ensuring that the cardio-respiratory, vascular and neuromuscular systems are adequately prepared.
- Level of arousal/motivation – ensuring that the performer is at their optimum level of arousal.
- Concentration / **selective attention** – particularly in simple reaction time situations, getting the performer to focus on the relevant stimulus and ignore everything else, for example, focusing on the gun in a sprint start.
- Improving physical fitness.
- Cue detection – analysing your opponents play so you can anticipate what they intend to do, for example, analysing opponents short and long serves in badminton.

Fig. 7.07 How response time can be improved.

Mental rehearsal

Selective attention

The above are also aided by anticipation, which is a very important method of improving both simple and choice reaction times. Anticipation comes in two forms.

Spatial	Temporal
Predicting *what* will happen, for example, a cricket batsman detecting the fast bowler's slower ball.	Predicting *when* it will happen, for example, the sprinter identifying the period of time between the 'set' and the gun going off.

Psychological refractory period (PRP)

For further information on the psychological refractory period, see p. 140 in *Advanced PE for OCR, AS*.

This is the negative side of anticipation. If we anticipate something and get it wrong, then our reactions are slower. If we detect a stimulus and are processing that information when a second stimulus arrives, we cannot attend to the second stimulus until we have finished processing the first. This delay makes our reaction time longer and the delay is known as the psychological refractory period (PRP).

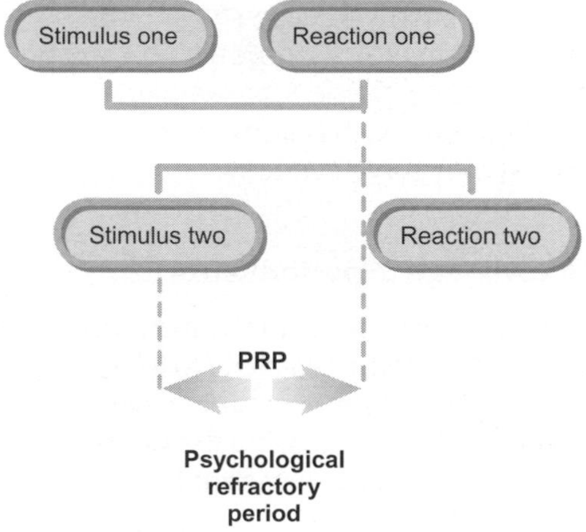

Fig. 7.08 The PRP is the delay caused by being able to process only one piece of information at a time.

For further information on feedback, see pp. 141–2 in *Advanced PE for OCR, AS*.

Feedback

4 Feedback

Feedback is the information received by the performer during the course of the movement or as a result of it. There are several different types of feedback.

Intrinsic	Extrinsic
Comes from the proprioceptors and kinaesthesis. Concerns the feel of the movement, for example, the feel of balance during a handstand. Very important for experienced performers, but novices need to be made aware of the need to develop this form of feedback.	Feedback from external sources, for example, teacher/coach. Received via sight and hearing, and is used to support intrinsic feedback. Very important for beginners.

As well as intrinsic and extrinsic feedback there is also:

Concurrent (continuous)	Terminal
Received during the movement. It is intrinsic and is generated by the proprioceptors/kinaesthesis, for example, gymnast knowing that they are balanced correctly.	Feedback given after the movement is completed or later, for example, coach discussing the match at the next training session. It is extrinsic.

Positive	Negative
The movement is successful and the feedback reinforces the learning. Can be intrinsic or extrinsic, for example, badminton coach praises performer when they serve correctly.	The movement is incorrect/unsuccessful and the feedback is used to make it successful. Can be intrinsic or extrinsic, for example, badminton serve lands outside service area.

Knowledge of performance	Knowledge of results
Concerns the quality of the movement. Can be external (from teachers/coaches) or internal from proprioceptors/kinaesthesis. Could be from discussing the performance or watching a video. Important for experienced performers.	Concerns the outcome of our movements and is extrinsic. It can be both positive and negative. Usually arises from teachers/ coaches actually seeing the result (ball going over the boundary for six), or watching the movement on video. Very important in the early stages of learning and for improving performance.

Why is feedback important?

- The performer knows what to do to improve.
- Correct actions are reinforced.
- Incorrect actions stopped and bad habits are prevented.
- Performer is motivated and their confidence is boosted.

Feedback should be:

- compared to previous performances
- related to/specific to the performance
- easily understood by the performer
- in manageable amounts for the performer to deal with
- linked to goals if it is to be effective.

CHECK !

Go back to the overview diagrams on pp. 51 and 65. If you are satisfied with your knowledge and understanding, tick off the sections that you have revised so far. If you are not satisfied, then revisit those sections and refer to the pages in the 'Need to know more?'

Exam practice

1 Whiting used this model to explain how physical movement occurs.

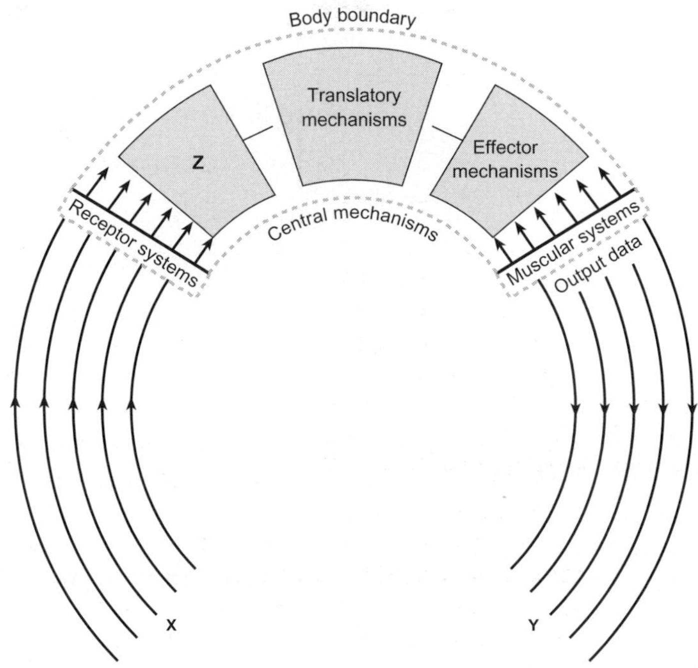

(a) Use a practical example to explain points X and Y on the diagram. (2 marks)

(b) The process occurring at point Z includes selective attention. Explain why selective attention is important to the short-term memory. (2 marks)

2 Define the terms 'reaction time', 'movement time' and 'response time' in relation to physical skills. (3 marks)

3 (a) Sketch and label a graph to illustrate Hick's Law. (2 marks)

(b) How does the number of choices available to a performer affect their performance? (1 mark)

4 How might you improve the reaction time of a performer in your chosen activity? (4 marks)

5 Describe the psychological refractory period (PRP). Use an example to show how it could be used to increase the reaction time of an opponent. (3 marks)

6 Feedback can affect motivation. What type of feedback is appropriate to motivate the novice and how might this change for the skilled player? (3 marks)

Now go to p. 154 to check your answers.

Chapter 8 **Control of motor skill in PE**

Chapter overview

Chapter 8: Control of motor skill in PE

1 Motor programmes ☐

2 Motor control ☐

3 Open loop and closed loop theory (Adams) ☐

4 Schema theory (Schmidt) ☐

For further information on control of motor skill in PE, see pp. 144–50 in *Advanced PE for OCR, AS.*

Tick the box when you are satisfied with your level of knowledge and understanding for each topic within this chapter.

1 Motor programmes

For further information on motor programmes, see pp. 144–5 in *Advanced PE for OCR, AS.*

Motor skills

Control

Executive motor programme (EMP)

Sub-routines

Over-learned

Hierarchical

Sequential

- **Motor skills** are physical actions.
- **Control** involves the manipulation and adjustment of movement to produce the required skill.
- A motor programme or **executive motor programme** (EMP) is an overall plan of the whole skill or pattern of movement.
- The plan is stored in the long-term memory (LTM).
- The plan is adjusted and updated each time the skill is performed.
- The EMP comprises **sub-routines.** These are mini skills often performed in sequence. Collectively they make up the whole skill.
- Sub-routines appear to be performed fluently and automatically when the skill has been grooved or **over-learned.**
- Automatic execution of skill takes place when the performer is at the expert stage.
- An expert is said to be at the autonomous phase of learning.

Figure 8.01 on the next page shows the **hierarchical** and **sequential** organization of a skill. Hierarchical means an order of importance. The EMP is more important than the supporting sub-routines. Sequential means that sub-routines are often performed in a particular order.

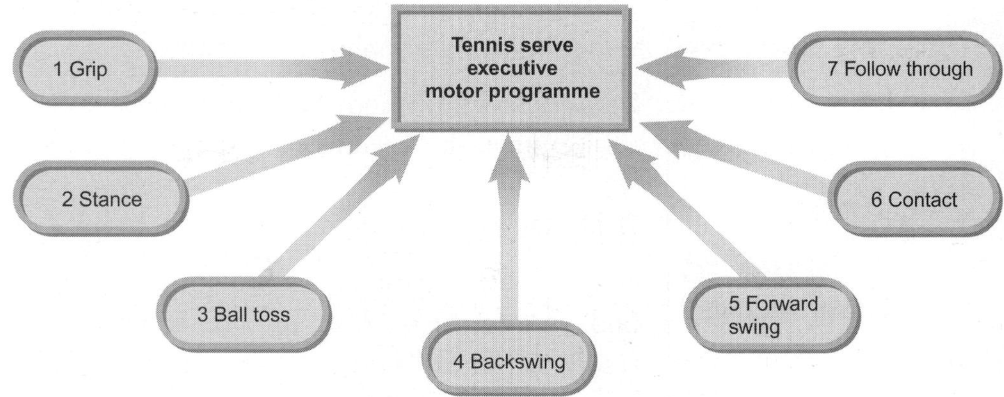

Fig. 8.01 Hierarchical and sequential organization of skill. A tennis serve is low in organization, note how each sub-routine is performed in sequence to make up the EMP.

Low organization

Low organization

- If a skill is low in organization, it can be divided easily into sub-routines, for example, throwing skills like the discus and javelin.
- Each sub-routine can be taught and practised separately. You need to learn three practice methods that can be used for a skill of low organization.

It is important to know that the classification and organization of skill determines the practice method used to teach and perfect the skill.

1. **Part practice:** each sub-routine is learned separately and in isolation until the whole skill has been put together.
2. **Progressive part practice:** two sub-routines are taught separately and then practised together before teaching a third sub-routine in isolation. The combination of three sub-routines is then practised as one skill.
3. **Whole-part-whole:** the skill is practised as a whole. One sub-routine is taken out and practised separately. The skill in then performed as a whole.

Part practice

Progressive part practice

Whole-part-whole

Backward chaining

Sub-routines, particularly in throwing skills, such as the javelin and discus, can often be taught in reverse order. This practice method is called **backward chaining.**

High organization

High organization

- If a skill is high in organization, it cannot be divided into sub-routines. One sub-routine cannot be taught as an isolated component.
- You need to learn two practice methods that can be used for a skill of high organization.

Whole practice

Task simplification

1 **Whole practice.** The skill is performed as a whole, for example, sprinting or dribbling a football.

2 **Task simplification.** Making the task easier than it really is, for example, short tennis simplifies the rudiments of the major game.

For further information on the organization of skill, see pp. 118–20 in *Advanced PE for OCR, AS*.

2 Motor control

Motor control involves manipulation and often the adjustment of the body during performance in order to bring about the desired response. An explanation of motor skill control is given in the **open loop** and **closed loop** theory.

It is essential the practice conditions replicate the conditions in which the skill is performed. The relationship between practice and performance in the real situation is termed 'transfer'. Positive transfer is a major learning process.

3 Open loop and closed loop theory (Adams)

This theory extends to three levels.

Level one – open loop

Motor command

The plan or EMP (stored in LTM)

The action of the movement effectors (working muscles)

Fig. 8.02 Open loop does not engage feedback.

Open loop is sometimes called a motor programme. One decision triggers an action that has been learned and stored. See autonomous Phase of Learning.

- The EMP is stored as an overall plan in the long-term memory.
- The EMP is triggered by the situation and is transferred almost spontaneously to the working muscle.
- The open loop is termed the **memory trace.**
- Its function is to produce the initial movement of the skill and no reference is made to feedback.
- For a skill of rapid execution, such as a golf drive, the movement is so rapid that feedback cannot be referenced after the swing has started.
- Open loop is associated with quick, dynamic and ballistic actions.
- Open loop is most likely to operate during closed skills.

Open loop

Closed loop

Memory trace

Levels two and three – closed loops

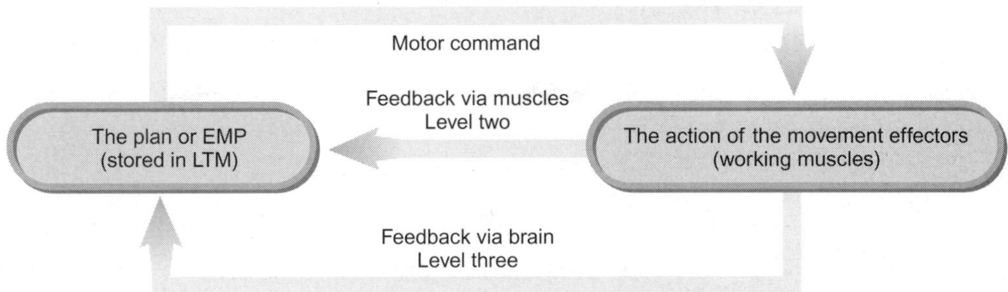

Fig. 8.03 Levels two and three involve feedback. Feedback completes or closes the loop.

- Level two operates on a short feedback loop and is a closed loop system of control.
- Control is achieved through **muscle reaction.**
- Without thinking, rapid adjustments can be made during performance. For example, the downhill skier makes **subconscious** alterations in order to retain balance.
- Adjustments are stored in the long-term memory.
- This feedback loop does not engage the central cognitive processes
- Its function is to complete the skill.

Muscle reaction

Perceptual trace

Subconscious

Level three

- Level three operates on a longer feedback loop because information is relayed back to the brain, which in turn processes performance modifications.
- Feedback is information about the performance and outcome of the skill.
- This process involves thought and greater attention is given to the plan.
- Adjustments are stored in the long-term memory as fresh motor programmes.
- Level three closed loop is called the **perceptual trace** and is frequently used in open skills requiring decision-making. For example, passing a ball in rugby demands conscious thought.
- Its function is to complete the skill.

The memory trace triggers the perceptual trace.

Most skills operate as a result of dual functioning of open and closed loops. This would explain control. Adjustments made because of feedback are stored as new EMP. This is one explanation about how learning takes place.

The perceptual trace operates as follows:

1 During performance, the perceptual trace compares the current action against the learned pattern of movement, which is stored in the long-term memory.

NEED TO KNOW MORE?

For further information on open loop and closed loop theory, see pp. 146–8 in *Advanced PE for OCR, AS*.

2 If the comparison matches, the skill is allowed to continue and is reinforced.
3 The action will be modified if a mismatch is detected.
4 Modifications are stored as fresh motor programmes.

Three drawbacks of open and closed theory are recognised:

KEY WORDS

Novel response

1 It would be impossible to store an infinite number of motor programmes.
2 If total retention/storage were possible, fast and accurate retrieval would be difficult.
3 The execution of a novel response could not happen because the necessary motor programme is not stored. A novel response is an unusual, improvised and often creative action.

4 Schema theory (Schmidt)

KEY WORDS

Generalized movements

Schema theory

Transfer

Schema theory provides a solution to the drawbacks above. It states that EMPs are not stored as separate plans as presented by open and closed loop theory, but are stored in the long-term memory as experiences or relationships with motor programmes.

- Schema is an accumulation of experiences.
- Experiences or relationships are termed **generalized movements.**
- Generalized movements are adaptations or modifications of movements that **transfer** to help with the learning and performance of other skills.

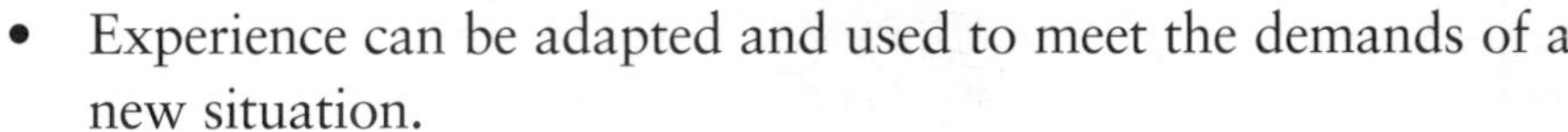

HOT TIPS

Be aware of the strong link between transfer and schema.

- Experience can be adapted and used to meet the demands of a new situation.
- The process of using previous experience to help with the learning of new skills, and even with the performance of over-learned skills, is called 'transfer'.

KEY WORDS

Four memory items

Experience is accumulated by gathering information from **four memory items.** Using an example of two attackers approaching one defender in rugby, these memory items are identified and explained below. The example relates specifically to the ball carrier.

NEED TO KNOW MORE?

For further information on Schema theory, see pp. 148–9 in *Advanced PE for OCR, AS*.

Type of schema	Four memory items	Explanation of memory items with a practical example
Recall schema Functions: to store information, to start the response.	**1** Knowledge of inital conditions	Refers to the environmental situation. For example, the player may have experienced a similar situation in a practice or a previous game.
	2 Knowledge of response specification	Refers to knowing what to do in this situation. For example, the well-timed pass may be the answer as it has been successful in previous similar situations.
Recognition schema Functions: to control the movement, to elevate the performance.	**3** Knowledge of sensory consequences	Refers to kinaesthesis. How much pressure or force to apply to the skill. For example, how hard should the ball be passed in this situation?
	4 Knowledge of outcome	Refers to knowing what the result of the skill is likely to be. For example, the well-timed pass makes it impossible for the defender to make a tackle.

CHECK !

Go back to the overview diagrams on pp. 51 and 76. If you are satisfied with your knowledge and understanding, tick off the sections that you have revised so far. If you are not satisfied, then revisit those sections and refer to the pages in the 'Need to know more?'

Exam practice

1 What is a motor programme? (1 mark)

2 How is a motor programme created and operated? (4 marks)

3 Below are four parameters of schema theory. Use a practical example to explain each of the parameters:

(a) initial conditions
(b) response specifications
(c) sensory consequences
(d) movement outcomes.

(4 marks)

4 By using practical examples, illustrate when it would be best to use whole practice as a teaching method. (3 marks)

5 Describe the practice method known as progressive part and explain, by using a practical example, how it could be used when teaching a motor skill in PE. (4 marks)

6 Describe the open loop theory of control and explain, by using a practical example, how it operates during a motor skill. (4 marks)

Now go to p. 156 to check your answers.

Chapter 9 **Learning skills in PE**

Chapter overview

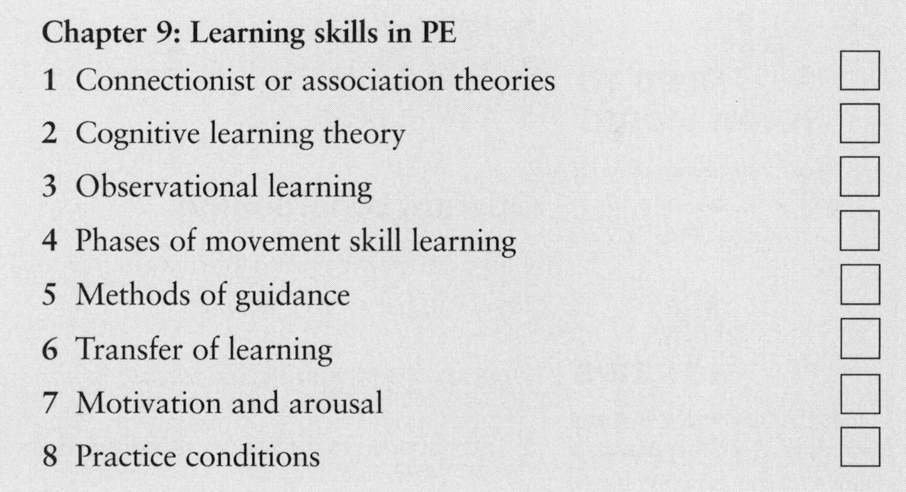

Chapter 9: Learning skills in PE

1 Connectionist or association theories ☐
2 Cognitive learning theory ☐
3 Observational learning ☐
4 Phases of movement skill learning ☐
5 Methods of guidance ☐
6 Transfer of learning ☐
7 Motivation and arousal ☐
8 Practice conditions ☐

For further information on learning skills in PE, see pp. 151–65 in *Advanced PE for OCR, AS.*

Tick the box when you are satisfied with your level of knowledge and understanding for each topic within this chapter.

S/R bond

Learning bond

Reinforcement

1 Connectionist or association theories

- This theory depends upon linking or connecting a stimulus with a response.
- This connection is termed an **S/R bond** or **learning bond.**
- S represents a stimulus, whilst R is the response.
- In the Hot Tip example, the response becomes connected or associated with the solution.
- The connection of S/R or learning bond is strengthened by the process of **reinforcement.**
- Reinforcement is the process causing behaviour to reoccur.
- The learning bond is stored in the long-term memory.

In the examination, you will be asked to give practical examples. Practical examples, when requested, are worth marks.

Reinforcement can be given in two ways.

A practical example of an S-R learning bond is as follows. A high cross coming towards the goalkeeper is a stimulus. The response or solution to the stimulus is to catch the ball. If the catch is successful the response connects with the stimulus and a learning bond has been formed.

1 Positive reinforcement involves the presentation of the stimulus of approval or a 'satisfier'. This could be in the form of verbal praise or a tangible reward.

2 Negative reinforcement involves the withdrawal of an aversive stimulus after behaviour has occurred, for example, criticism is withdrawn following a desired response.

HOT TIPS

It is important to be aware that both forms of reinforcement serve to strengthen the learning bond.

NEED TO KNOW MORE?

For further information on Thorndyke's Laws, see p. 151 in *Advanced PE for OCR, AS*.

HOT TIPS

Students often neglect to revise Thorndyke's Laws. They provide a key area in connectionist theory.

Operant conditioning is the only connectionist theory about which you have to know. You need to know five points about it.

Practical examples are required in the examination. These are given on pp. 151–3 in *Advanced PE for OCR, AS*.

KEY WORDS

Problem solving

Cognitive

HOT TIPS

Be aware that cognitive learning theory states that learning is most effective when the learner is presented with a whole problem to solve and is not efficiently accomplished by connecting learning bonds, which only relate to parts of the whole problem.

Although learning can take place in different ways a psychologist named Thorndyke believed that the most effective way to learn was to form and strengthen a learning bond through the application of reinforcement. Thorndyke presented three laws that relate to application of reinforcement.

1 Law of Effect
2 Law of Exercise
3 Law of Readiness.

Operant conditioning

This is a major connectionist theory and was presented by a psychologist called Skinner.

Operant conditioning involves:

1 structuring a situation to bring about a desired response
2 trial and error learning
3 reinforcement of the response
4 changing the response
5 the process of changing the response is termed 'behaviour shaping'.

2 Cognitive learning theory

- Gestalt theory is the major cognitive theory.
- Two psychologists, Werthheimer and Kohler, believed that learning is most effective through **problem solving**.
- This approach is in direct contrast to the connectionist belief.
- A **cognitive** process is a thinking process.

For learning to take place when cognitive theory is applied, five factors must be in place.

1 Perception. This is interpretation or understanding of the whole task, for example, difficulty encountered in the execution of a vault may be eased if the gymnast is made aware of the mechanics of the movement.
2 Previous experience. Related experience can help to establish insight as to how the new task is to be performed, for example, the experience of throwing a ball relates to the learning of a service in tennis (transfer of learning).
3 Current knowledge. The learner needs an insight as to what is required, for example, what strategies are required to defeat a full court press in basketball.

Cognitive theory involves a period of purposeful experimentation in which the learner uses experience, knowledge and perception to solve the whole problem.

Mechanical guidance

For further information on cognitive learning theory and the contrast with connectionist theory, see p. 153 in *Advanced PE for OCR, AS.*

For further information on observational learning, see pp. 153–4 in *Advanced PE for OCR, AS.*

4 Motivation. The learner must be motivated to solve the problem.

5 Self-esteem. Learning by the cognitive learning theory can be accomplished only if the novice has a positive self-perception.

- Gestalt is a philosophy, which refers to temporal patterning.
- The Gestaltian belief is that the whole problem is greater than the sum of the parts; that is, learning is best accomplished by presenting the whole problem as opposed to presenting parts of the problem.
- In practice terms, this means that skills are best learned through conditioned or adapted games rather than trying to perfect techniques in isolation from the game.
- **Mechanical guidance** can be used to simplify the whole skill. For example, a tumbling harness can help the learning of a somersault in trampolining or a buoyancy aid can help the novice swimmer to experience the 'feeling tone' of the whole stroke.
- The solution to the whole problem may emerge suddenly. This is called the 'eureka phenomenon'.

3 Observational learning

A psychologist named Bandura believed that learning was most effectively achieved by imitating or copying from others. Observational learning theory involves watching a demonstration and replicating the model. The learner must display four factors before learning can be achieved by way of observation.

1. Attention. The learner is required to focus concentration onto the model.
2. Retention. The learner must remember the image.
3. Motor reproduction. The learner must have the necessary ability and skill to replicate the demonstration.
4. Motivation. The learner must have the drive to learn.

4 Phases of movement skill learning

Two psychologists, Fitts and Posner, presented three learning phases or stages. They relate directly to the acquisition of motor skills.

The cognitive phase

- The thinking stage. The learner engages in mental rehearsal and would benefit from observing a demonstration.

- By the end of this phase the learner would attempt to perform the skill.
- Feedback needs to be both extrinsic and positive to highlight errors in performance.

HOT TIPS

Do not confuse cognitive learning theory with the cognitive stage of learning. Although they sound similar, they are unrelated and students often confuse them.

The associative phase

- The practice stage in which the learner participates physically.
- The response is inefficient and often incorrect.
- The learner requires great concentration during performance.
- Mental rehearsal can help learning and develop fluency.
- Demonstration remains important whilst reinforcement should be positive.
- Control of the skill is largely through external feedback (KR)
- The learner begins to use intrinsic or kinaesthetic feedback (KP) to control the skill.

The autonomous phase

NEED TO KNOW MORE?

For further information on stages of learning, see pp. 155–6 in *Advanced PE for OCR, AS*.

- The expert stage as the skill can be executed automatically.
- The movement has been 'grooved' or over-learned.
- The correct response can now be associated with the correct 'feeling tone'.
- Attention can be given to peripheral environmental cues.
- Demonstration and mental rehearsal remain important.
- The expert uses intrinsic feedback for self-correction (KP).
- Negative extrinsic feedback from the coach assists fault correction and helps in fine tuning.

5 Methods of guidance

There are four types of guidance, which can be used to help the learning process.

HOT TIPS

Visual guidance is best used at the cognitive stage of learning, whilst verbal guidance can be used to good affect during the autonomous stage of learning.

1. Visual guidance. This can be in the form of a demonstration or display changes, for example, chalking the floor during tennis serving practice to give the learner a target.
2. Verbal guidance. This involves telling the learner what to do. It has more benefit to the learning of open skills, which require decision-making and perceptual judgements.
3. Manual guidance. The coach would hold and physically manipulate the body to give the learner an idea of how the skill should feel.
4. Mechanical guidance. This makes use of an object or piece of apparatus to shape the skill, for example the tackle bag in rugby.

For further information on methods of guidance, see pp. 156–7 in *Advanced PE for OCR, AS*.

For the examination, you need to be aware of the link between schema theory and transfer. Schema is an accumulation of knowledge and motor programmes, which can be adapted and transferred to help a response to a new situation. An adaptation is termed a 'generalization'.

Positive transfer

Negative transfer

Proactive transfer

Retroactive transfer

Bilateral transfer

For further information on types of transfer, see pp. 159–60 in *Advanced PE for OCR, AS*.

All learning is based on transfer, consider fundamental patterns of movement (FPMs) to executive motor programmes. See pages 125–6 in *Advanced PE for OCR, AS*.

Both manual and mechanical guidance have drawbacks, such as:

- the learning becomes reliant on the type of guidance
- these types of guidance are not given in the real game situation. Therefore, overuse of manual and mechanical guidance could result in negative transfer.

6 Transfer of learning

Transfer is a process of one skill influencing the learning and performance of a separate skill. This is an important topic as practically all learning is based on some form of transfer.

You need to learn five types of transfer in the context of practical application.

1 **Positive transfer** occurs when one skill helps the learning and performance of another, for example, throwing helps the racquet arm action in tennis serving.

2 **Negative transfer** is evident when one skill impedes the learning and performance of another, for example, the wrist actions in tennis and badminton are completely different.

3 **Proactive transfer** takes place when a previously learned skill influences the learning and performance of a new skill either positively or negatively, for example, learning to throw overarm as a child will later help the racquet arm action when learning to serve in tennis.

4 **Retroactive transfer** occurs when new skills influence the learning and performance of old skills either positively or negatively, for example, learning a tennis serve as a student may influence throwing skills acquired in childhood.

5 **Bilateral transfer** is the transfer of learning from limb to limb, for example, a dominant right footed player learning to kick with the left.

It is useful to be aware that there are other types of transfer:

- transfer appropriate processing
- principle to skill
- near transfer
- far transfer
- ability to skill
- practice to performance.

For further information on motivation and arousal, see pp. 160–4 in *Advanced PE for OCR, AS.*

Motivation

Arousal

7 Motivation and arousal

Motivation is the psychological drive to succeed. **Arousal** is the degree of excitement or activation that prepares the person for performance.

Learning and the performance of motor skills cannot take place without a degree of motivation. There are two types of motivation.

1 Intrinsic motivation is the drive from within, for example, to achieve mastery for its own sake.
2 Extrinsic motivation is when motivation comes from some outside source, for example, an award or trophy. Extrinsic reward is a valuable motivator for a beginner, but will eventually undermine intrinsic motivation.

Motivation has two components:

- intensity of behaviour is the degree of physical and emotional energy displayed by the individual. This is known as arousal.
- Direction of behaviour is the way arousal is used to reach a goal or target.

You need to learn three theories relating to motivation and arousal.

Drive theory

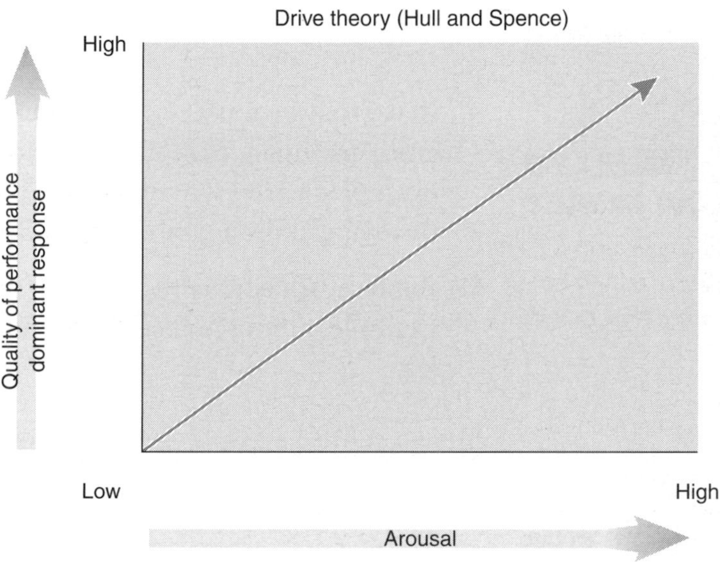

Fig. 9.01 Drive theory.

Understanding the implications of Drive theory for teaching and learning is important for the exam.

- Drive theory indicates that as arousal increases, there is a proportional increase in the quality of performance.

Dominant responses

- The quality of performance depends upon how well the skill has been learned.
- Actions that have been learned are called **dominant responses.**
- Dominant responses are the actions that are most likely to occur as arousal increases.

The implications for teaching and learning are:

- at the associative phase of learning, the dominant response is likely to be incorrect. Therefore, the novice learns best when in a condition of low arousal.
- at the autonomous phase of learning, the dominant response is likely to be fluent and correct. Therefore, the expert would perform better in an environment that stimulates high arousal.

Inverted U theory

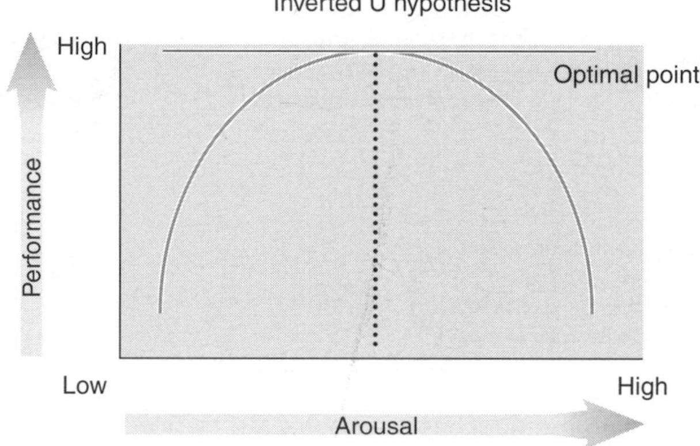

Fig. 9.02 Inverted U theory.

HOT TIPS

The capacity to concentrate and perform the skill correctly directly influences the potential to learn.

- Inverted U theory predicts that as arousal increases, the quality of performance and the capacity to concentrate improves to be at their best at the optimal point.
- The optimal point is also called the 'threshold of arousal' and occurs mid way along the arousal axis.
- After the optimal point, if arousal continues to increase, the capacity to perform and concentrate will decline.

Link the inverted U theory to Information processing, page 129 in *Advanced PE for OCR, AS*.

The implications for teaching and learning are:

Under-arousal

- Attention field (the environment of which we are aware) widens excessively.
- The learner will not be able to selectively attend to the most relevant cues.
- Information overload or an excessive amount of incoming information will result.

Selective attention cannot operate when under- or over-aroused.

Over-arousal

Hypervigilance

- Attention field narrows excessively causing the relevant cues to be missed.
- In this condition, the learner may be experiencing high anxiety or panic.
- The technical term for this condition is **hypervigilance.**

Optimal arousal

Cue utilization

- Attention field adjusts to the ideal width.
- Learner is able to selectively attend to the relevant environmental cues and therefore process information efficiently. This process is termed **cue utilization.**
- Concentration is at a maximum.

Drive reduction theory

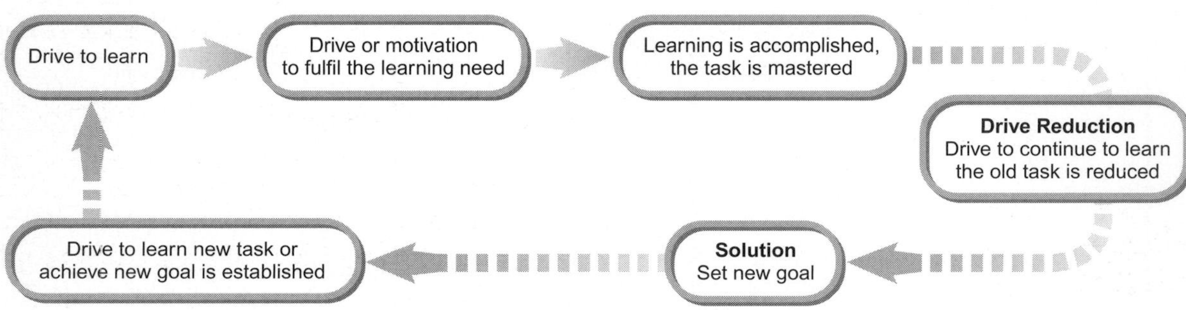

Fig. 9.03 When the learning goal has been achieved, the desire to continue with the same task decreases. The dotted line implies a new task or goal should be introduced.

The initial drive to learn the skill is strong, but once the skill is learned, this drive is reduced and as a result, the performance quality of the skill will decline.

The implications for teaching and learning are:

- the drive to learn must be maintained
- to replenish the drive, new targets should be introduced
- drive reduction could occur because of boredom through repetition
- practices should vary.

Strategies to increase the motivation to learn include:

Variability of practice

- positively reinforce the learner's performance
- provide extrinsic reward
- targets in learning should be challenging and realistic
- the practice or drill to attain a specific goal should be changed appropriately. This is called **variability of practice**

For further information on theories of arousal, see pp. 161–4 in *Advanced PE for OCR, AS*.

- make use of role models
- the teacher should present the skill as being a worthwhile element to learn
- the learner should be aware as to how progressions can be made
- practices should be fun.

Review discrete and continuous tasks, see page 114 in *Advanced PE for OCR, AS*.

8 Practice conditions

You need to learn two practice conditions.

1 Massed practice. This is a practice session with no breaks. It is used when the task is classified as simple and/or discrete. It can also be used when the motivation and ability of the group is high.

2 Distributed practice. This practice includes breaks and therefore the session is divided into shorter periods. It is used when the task is complex and classified as continuous, and the ability of the group is low.

For further information on practice conditions, see pp. 164–5 in *Advanced PE for OCR, AS*.

KEY WORDS

Mental rehearsal

Advantages of practice conditions	
Massed practice	**Distributed practice**
More physical work is possible in one session.	Allows periods of rest.
Allows the learner to experience the flow of the whole skill.	Feedback and performance analysis can be given.
Good for the development of kinaesthesis.	Enables the learner to engage in **mental rehearsal**.

Distributed practice is more effective than massed practice in the learning of motor skills.

CHECK !

Go back to the overview diagrams on pp. 51 and 83. If you are satisfied with your knowledge and understanding, tick off the sections that you have revised so far. If you are not satisfied, then revisit those sections and refer to the pages in the 'Need to know more?'

Mental rehearsal creates a picture of the skill in the mind of the performer. It is important to know that mental rehearsal is an important learning process. It is equal in importance to physical practice. Although the process stimulates tiny muscle movement, the major value of mental rehearsal is to serve a perceptual function.

Exam practice

1 Explain the cognitive learning theory and apply this to a practical situation. (4 marks)

2 Identify the three stages of learning and explain the type of feedback that would be effective at each stage. (3 marks)

3 What is an S/R bond and how can a PE teacher ensure that it is strengthened when teaching swimming or athletics? (3 marks)

4 Identify and explain three types of transfer that could be used in a PE lesson. (3 marks)

5 How could a PE teacher ensure positive transfer of learning in sports skills? (3 marks)

6 Use Bandura's model of observational learning to illustrate how the learning and performance of a named motor skill can be affected by using demonstration. (4 marks)

Now go to p. 158 to check your answers.

Unit 3: Contemporary studies in PE

Unit overview

Unit 3: Contemporary studies in PE

Tick the box when you are satisfied with your level of knowledge and understanding within each chapter.

Chapter 10 **PE and sport in schools**

Chapter overview

Chapter 10: PE and sport in school

1 PE in schools ☐

2 Sport in schools ☐

For further information on PE and sport in school, see pp. 166–87 in *Advanced PE for OCR, AS*.

Tick the box when you are satisfied with your level of knowledge and understanding for each topic within this chapter.

1 PE in schools

When looking at the various **concepts** (ideas or theories) in our **field of study** (focus area), it is useful to ask the following questions:

Concepts

Field of study

Leisure

- *who* is taking part – adults or children?
- *when* is it happening – fixed time or more flexible time?
- *where* is it taking place – purpose-built arena or more informal space?
- *why* are the participants involved – intrinsic or extrinsic reasons?
- *how* is it being pursued – high or low levels of organization, seriousness, fitness, commitment, and so on?

Leisure

For further information on leisure, see pp. 169–71 in *Advanced PE for OCR, AS*.

Leisure is a time when there is an opportunity for choice.

Leisure is an 'umbrella term' because all other concepts within our field of study (for example, play, physical recreation, PE and sport) can be part of it. These other concepts are either pursued in leisure time or (in the case of PE) prepare for active leisure.

When should a particular activity be classed as leisure?

- Consider the state of mind, or attitude, of the participant. For some, an activity, such as gardening, is a chosen, enjoyable leisure activity, while for others it is an unwelcome chore. Equally, football can be pursued as a leisure activity but for some people it is their work.

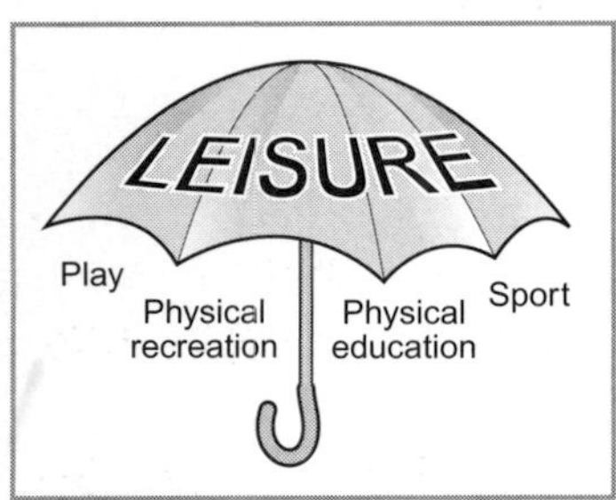

Fig. 10.01 Field of study.

- It is useful to consider leisure as an experience and to consider activities as the vehicle through which individuals experience leisure.

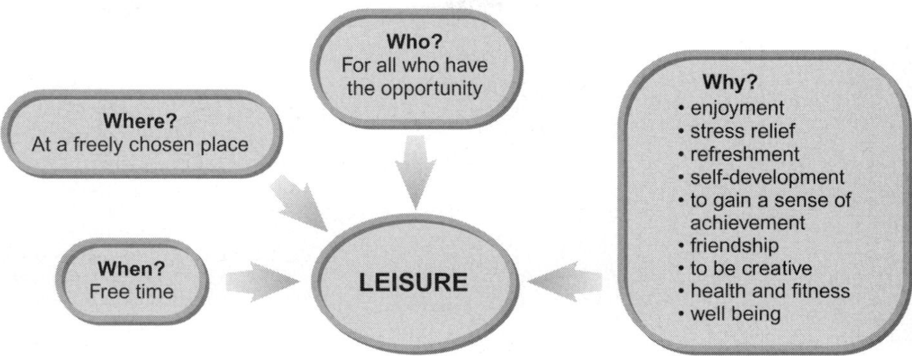

Fig. 10.02 Leisure.

HOT TIPS

Remember that leisure is an experience as well as an activity.

Our field of study can also be illustrated on a continuum (imaginary scale) showing varying levels of:

- organization
- spontaneity
- skilfulness
- commitment
- fitness.

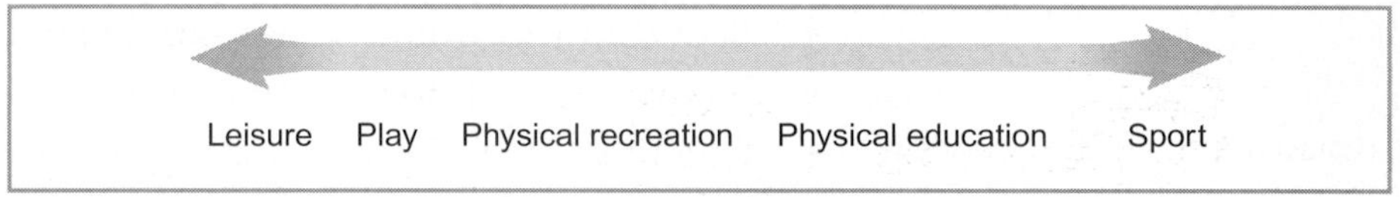

Fig. 10.03 The continuum between leisure and sport.

KEY WORDS

Play

Play

Play is a spontaneous, enjoyable, child-like activity.

Does play always have the characteristics shown in figure 10.04?

- Is it always fun? Not when there are arguments or injuries.
- Is it always spontaneous? Not when there are pre-arranged rules or time limits.
- Is the place for play always agreed by the participants? Not when restrictions are imposed by authority figures.

NEED TO KNOW MORE?

For further information on play, see pp. 172–5 in *Advance PE for OCR, AS*.

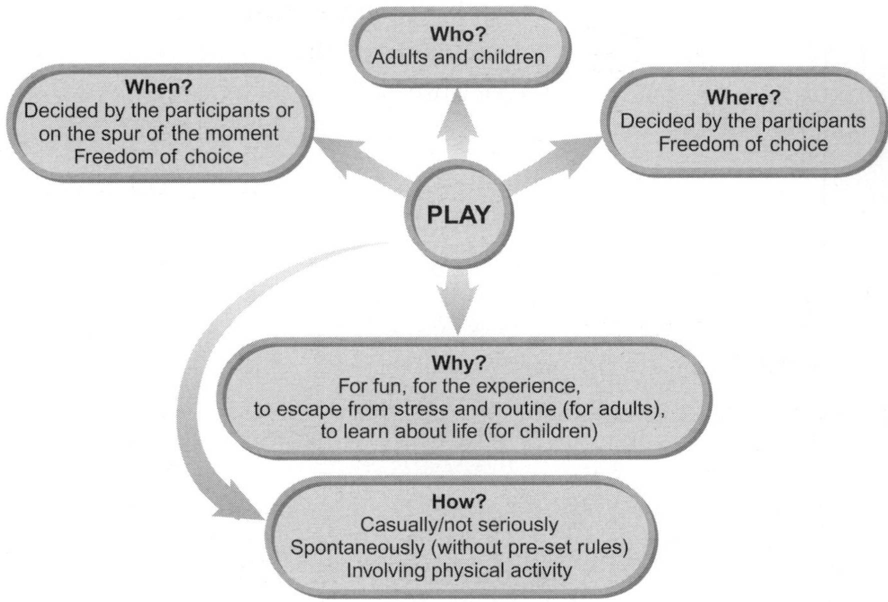

Fig. 10.04 Play.

- Is the time for play always agreed by participants? Not when restrictions are imposed by school times, meal times, and so on.
- Is play always casual/non-serious? No, as children can have very elaborate games that are taken very seriously.

An exam question may ask for characteristics of play **or** for situations when those characteristics may not be evident.

Values of play

- Physical, for example, skipping, hopping, jumping.
- Social, for example, co-operation, friendships.
- Moral, for example, being fair, being kind, not cheating.
- Environmental, for example, safety, caring for the environment.
- Cognitive, for example, making games, rules and decisions.
- Emotional, for example, managing both winning and losing properly.

Fig. 10.05 Play for adults and children.

Physical education

Physical education

Physical education can be described as:

- the formal teaching of both knowledge and values
- education of and through the physical.

For further information on physical education, see pp. 175–8 in *Advanced PE for OCR, AS*.

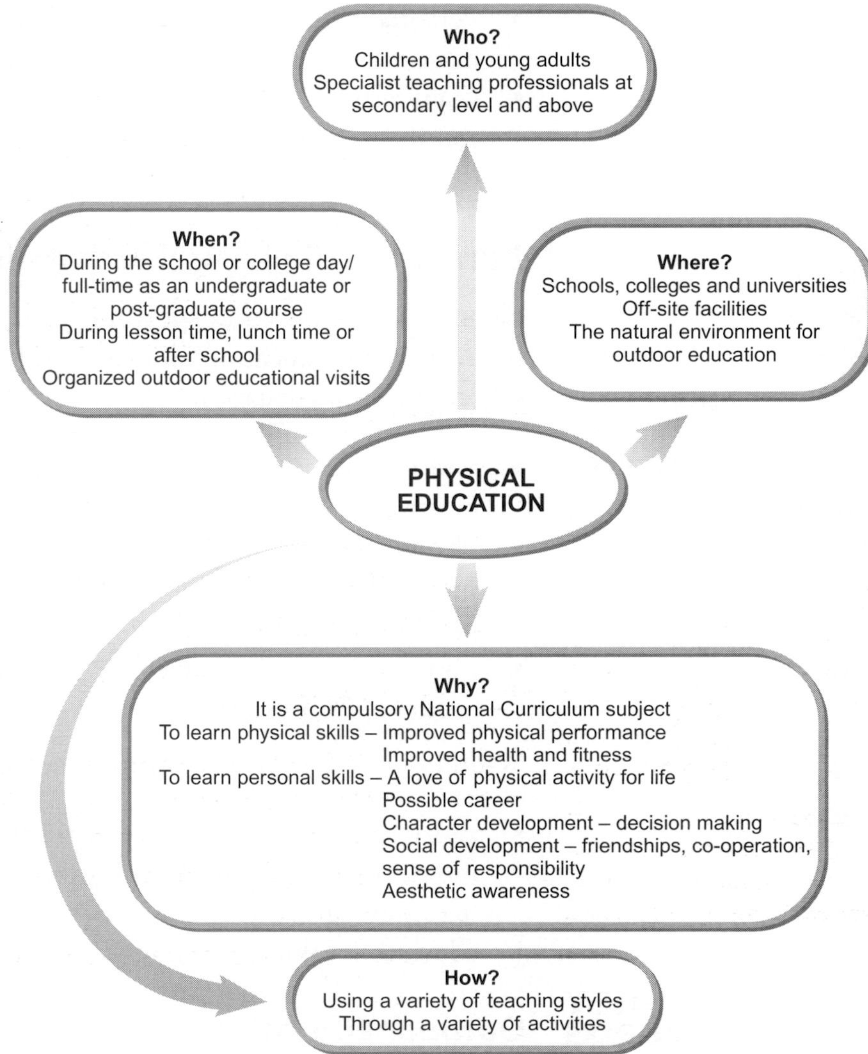

Fig. 10.06 Physical education.

Characteristics of physical education

- It is physical – children learn skills that enable them to take part in a variety of practical, recreative and/or sporting activities.
- It is child-centred – the child is more important than the activity or outcome.
- It is institutional – it takes place in educational establishments.
- It is valuable – children learn both physical and personal skills through PE.

Be sure that you understand and can give examples of the values of PE.

Values associated with physical education

- Physical values – those that improve health and motor skills, for example, cardiovascular fitness or agility.
- Preparation values – those that prepare for active leisure or a career, for example, gaining a love of gymnastics or wanting to become a PE teacher.
- Personal values – those that develop personal and social skills, for example, co-operation, leadership or confidence.
- Qualitative values – those that improve the quality of life, for example, an aesthetic awareness, an experience of achieving excellence.

Dimension of physical activity in schools

Figure 10.06 shows that sport, physical recreation and education all exist within school physical education.

You could be asked to explain how education, recreation and sport can all exist within a school PE programme, or how they each exist within one specific lesson. You could be given the diagram to help jog your memory, but not necessarily.

- Sport – competitive, extra-curricular or inter-house competitions.
- Physical recreation – enjoyment orientated, participation by all, perhaps in lunchtime clubs.
- Education – the learning that occurs in PE lessons.

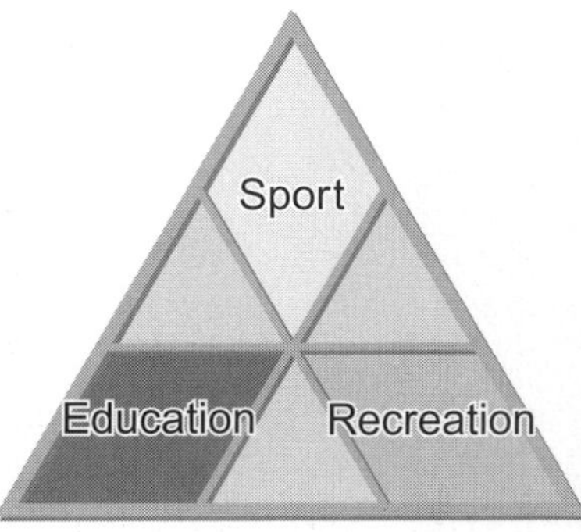

Fig. 10.07 Dimensions of physical activity in school.

Within one lesson of, for example, swimming:

- sport – the competitive race at the end of the lesson
- physical recreation – the enjoyable, fun orientated warm up or 'free time' at the end.
- education – the stroke analysis of the main body of the lesson.

Outdoor education

Outdoor education

Outdoor education can be described as learning in and about the outdoors.

It is the element of risk and the unpredictability of the natural environment that distinguishes outdoor education from others aspects of PE. It gives a unique opportunity for learning.

For further information on outdoor recreation, see pp. 179–81 in *Advanced PE for OCR, AS*.

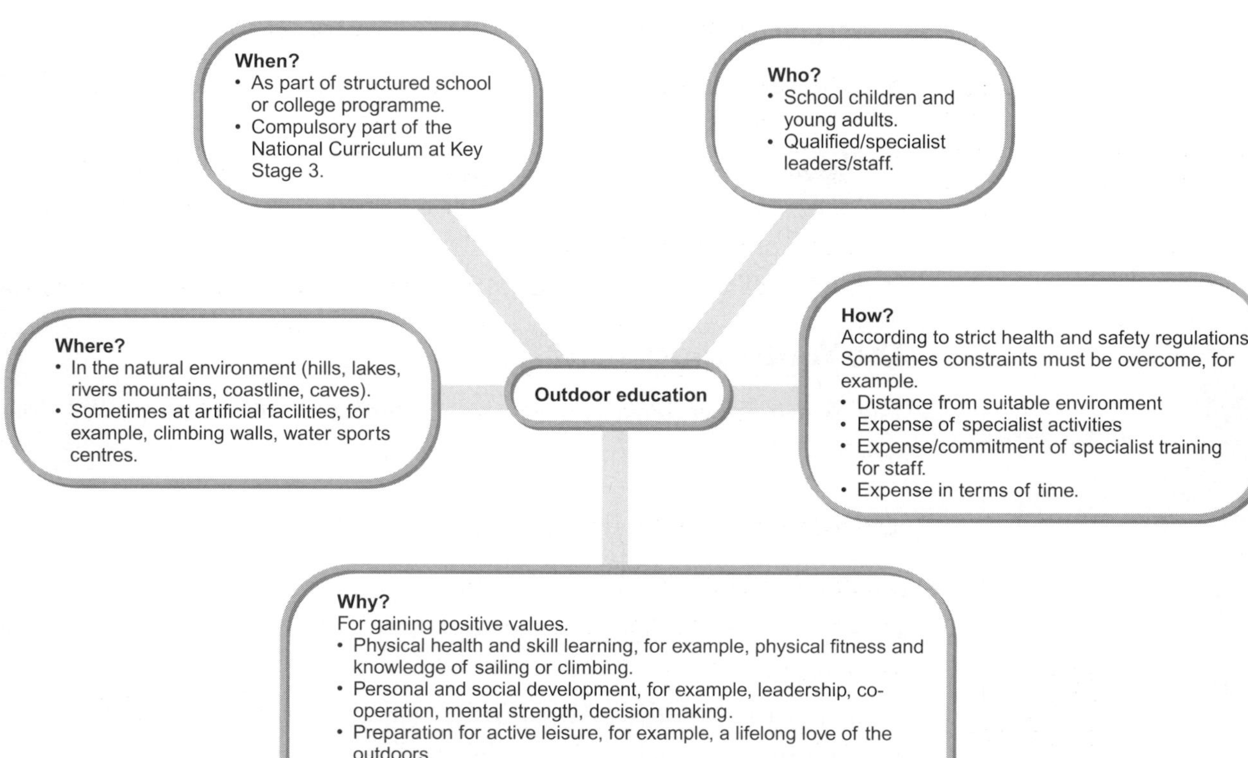

Fig. 10.08 Outdoor education.

HOT TIPS

Remember that outdoor education and outdoor recreation use the natural environment, for example, hills and rivers for learning and/or relaxing. They are not just playing games such as hockey outside.

Remember that outdoor pursuits can give personal challenge, develop awareness and respect for the countryside, teach people to work effectively with and depend on each other, and provide a sense of adventure or excitement.

Predictable Largely under the control of participant, for example, by correct use of equipment	**Unpredictable** Events over which participant has no control, for example, avalanche, flash flood, rock fall
Beginners	**Committed experts**
Perceived risk (imagined risk) Sought by teachers to give beginners/learners a sense of adventure and opportunities for personal challenge/development	**Real risk** (which can be dangerous or even fatal) Avoided at all costs by staff for youngsters/beginners by careful preparation and use of appropriate kit and equipment. Sometimes embraced by committed experts seeking greater challenges

Fig. 10.09 Risk factors in outdoor education.

2 Sport in schools

Sport in schools is currently promoted:

- at primary level – in England through the TOPS programmes (notably TOP Sport) and in Wales through Dragon Sport
- at secondary level – by specialist Sports Colleges
- at both levels – by sports development officers.

For further information about sport in schools, see pp. 181–7 in *Advanced PE for OCR, AS*.

The Youth Sport Trust

The Youth Sport Trust is a registered charity established in 1994. Its aim is to 'build a brighter future for young people through sport'.

It believes that all young people have the right to:

- an enjoyable experience of PE and sport
- a quality introduction to PE and sport suited to their own level of development
- a structured pathway of sporting opportunities
- high quality teaching, coaching and resources
- experience and benefit from positive competition
- develop a healthy lifestyle
- a foundation for lifetime physical activity.

Fig. 10.10 Youth Sport Trust.

Make sure that you can comment on the advantages (and if possible any potential disadvantages) of initiatives for sport in schools.

How does it operate and what does it do?

- It works with other organizations to develop and implement PE and sport programmes for young people.
- It is involved in the School Sport Co-ordinator programme.
- It is contracted by the Department for Education and Skills (DfES) to provide help and advice for schools applying for Sports College status and to give ongoing support as these colleges implement their development plan.
- It has developed the TOP programmes.
- It has also developed projects which focus on specific issues, such as:
  - inclusion of young disabled people
  - encouraging more teenage girls to take part in sport
  - tackling social exclusion within primary schools through playground development
  - supporting gifted and talented young sports people.

School sports co-ordinators work to raise participation and performance by facilitating a partnership plan. The partnership often revolves around a sports college and includes secondary schools and their associated 'feeder' schools.

You will not get a question specifically on the School Sports Co-ordinator programme, but you may be able to mention it and get credit for it in an answer to a question on initiatives in school.

For further information about school sports co-ordinators, see pp. 185–5 in *Advanced PE for OCR, AS*.

TOP Sport

- TOP Sport is one of the TOP programmes.
- The TOP programmes are a series of linked and progressive schemes for young people aged eighteen months to eighteen years.
- The programmes include TOP Tots (eighteen months to three years), TOP Start (three to five year olds), TOP Play (four to nine year olds), TOP Sport, TOP Skill (eleven to fourteen year olds), TOP Link (fourteen to sixteen year olds), and TOP Sportsability (young people with disabilities).
- Since their launch in 1994 the TOP programmes have reached over 30,000 schools and pre-school groups, every LEA and local authority sport and recreation unit and over 30,000 teachers and deliverers.

Fig. 10.11 TOP Sport.

TOP Sport

- It is for seven to eleven year olds.
- It provides opportunities for young people to develop skills in a range of sports.
- Programme delivery is also supported by the Sports Council for Northern Ireland and sportscotland.
- It is run in partnership with LEAs/schools/local authority sports development officers/NGBs/sports clubs.
- It supports the National Curriculum.

Key features of the TOP programmes include:

- illustrated resource cards
- child-friendly equipment
- quality training for teachers and deliverers.

The TOP programmes also run in Scotland and Northern Ireland.

Dragon Sport

Fig. 10.12 Dragon Sport.

- A scheme to give seven to eleven year olds regular, well-organized and enjoyable sporting experiences.
- Based on New Zealand's Kiwi Sport.
- Supported by the Youth Sport Trust.
- Resources and training are based on TOP Sport.

Its aims are:

- to develop strong school/club links
- to support the development of junior sections by clubs

- to encourage parents, teachers and other adults to get involved in sports leadership
- to give seven to eleven year olds a good sporting experience.

It provides:

- resource cards
- equipment bags
- training.

HOT TIPS

You could get a choice within a question, for example, 'Comment on the advantages of either TOP Sport or Sports Colleges'.

Sports Colleges

Sports Colleges and School Sport Co-ordinators are central to a growing network of sporting communities.

Sports Colleges are:

- part of the government's specialist schools programme
- hub sites for school and community sport
- regional focal points for excellence in PE and sport
- the central focus of the School Sport Co-ordinator programme.

They aim to:

- provide high quality teaching in PE and sport
- increase opportunities for gifted and talented performers
- give access to sports-specific qualifications, for example, AS and A Level PE
- develop sporting opportunities in the community
- link with local schools.

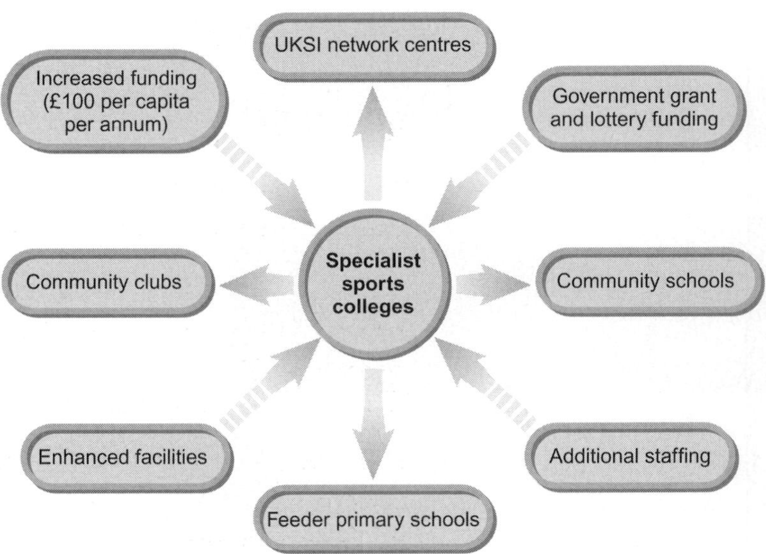

Fig. 10.13 The ins and outs of specialist Sports Colleges.

Sports Development Officers (SDOs)

- Employees of the local authority.
- Part of a county Sports Development Unit.
- Usually work with all sports but sometimes sport specific (SSDOs).

What do they do?

HOT TIPS

Carefully learn what the Youth Sport Trust, TOP Sport (Dragon Sport), Sports Colleges and Sports Development Officers do for sport in schools.

- Work to increase community access to sport and leisure.
- Work to increase opportunity and provision.
- Provide advice, support and resources to performers, coaches and clubs.
- Promote Sport England's Active Sports Programme.
- Develop 'Coaching for Teachers'.
- Organize sports festivals and courses.
- Help set up clubs.
- Advise on lottery and specialist Sports College applications.
- Work with county, borough and district leisure services departments.
- Work with schools, colleges and universities.

CHECK !

Go back to the overview diagrams on pp. 93 and 94. If you are satisfied with your knowledge and understanding, tick off the sections that you have revised so far. If you are not satisfied, then revisit those sections and refer to the pages in the 'Need to know more?'

Exam practice

1 Why is it that for some people sport is part of their leisure, yet for others it is their work? (5 marks)

2 PE is a compulsory school subject. Identify and give examples of three different types of values that can be gained from PE. (6 marks)

3 Specialist Sports Colleges are part of the government's specialist schools programme.
What are the aims of specialist Sports Colleges? (4 marks)

4 TOP Sport in England and Dragon Sport in Wales are initiatives to improve sport in primary schools. Describe the TOP Sport or the Dragon Sport programme. (5 marks)

Now go to p. 161 to check your answers.

Chapter 11 **Concepts of sport in society**

Chapter overview

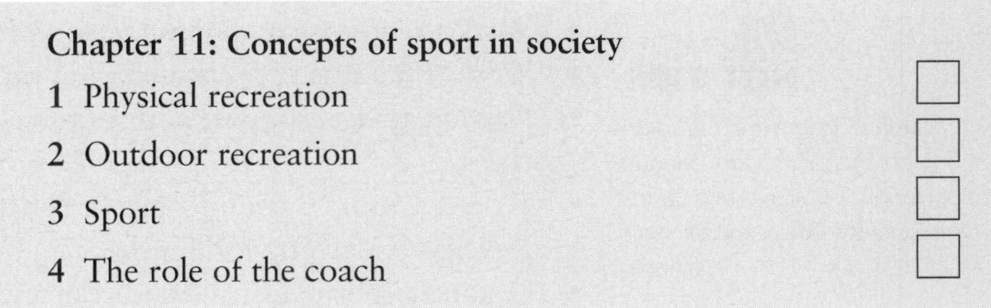

Chapter 11: Concepts of sport in society

1 Physical recreation ☐
2 Outdoor recreation ☐
3 Sport ☐
4 The role of the coach ☐

For further information on concepts of sport in society, see pp. 188–99 in *Advanced PE for OCR, AS*.

Tick the box when you are satisfied with your level of knowledge and understanding for each topic within this chapter.

1 Physical recreation

When an activity is pursued as physical recreation, the emphasis is on:

- taking part rather than winning
- having a good experience rather than strictly sticking to National Governing Body rules
- personal satisfaction rather than record breaking
- enjoyment rather than competition.

For further information on the concept of physical recreation, see pp. 188–190 in *Advanced PE for OCR, AS*.

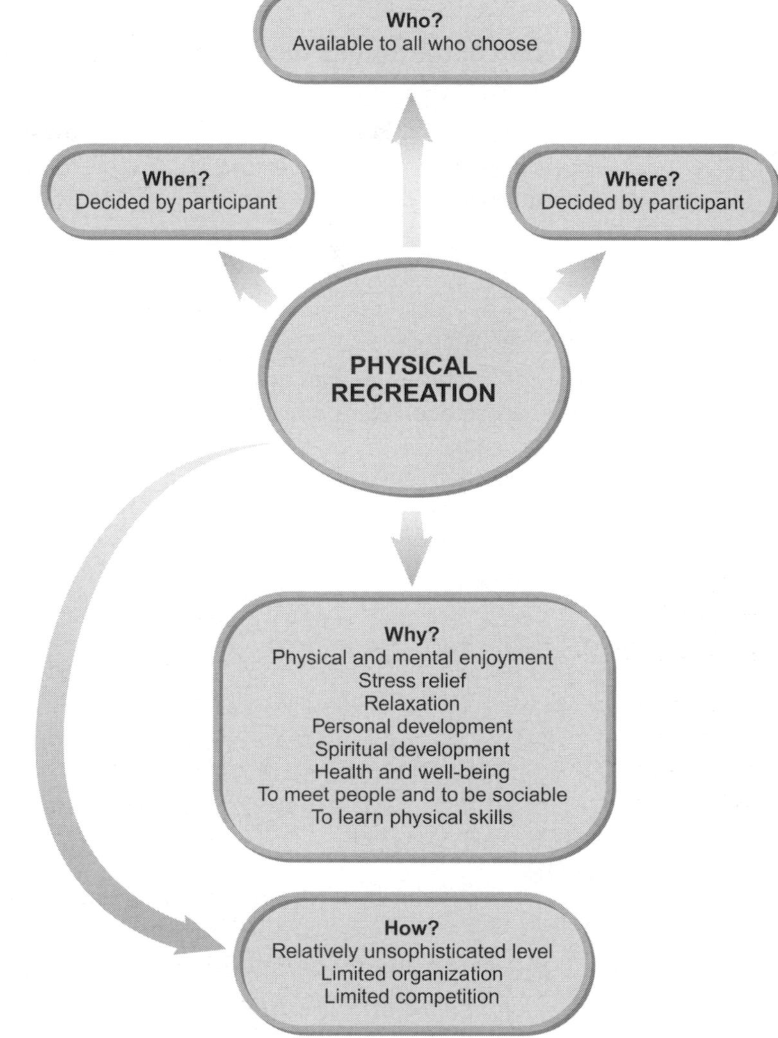

Fig. 11.01 Physical recreation.

HOT TIPS

Note that many characteristics of physical recreation overlap with characteristics of play. Some people say that physical recreation implies 'adults at play!'

2 Outdoor recreation

NEED TO KNOW MORE?

For further information on outdoor recreation, see pp. 190–192 in *Advanced PE for OCR, AS*.

Outdoor recreation is the use of the natural environment (mountains, forests, rivers, hills, coastline, and so on) for enjoyment during leisure time.

Outdoor recreation can develop the following:

Appreciation of the natural environment	Respect for the countryside
Getting 'back to nature' can: • relieve stress • lead to a greater appreciation of 'the great outdoors'.	• Enjoyable outdoor recreation experiences can develop a greater desire to preserve the countryside. • Some may get involved in green/ conservation and/or pollution issues.

A sense of adventure	An awareness of risk and safety
• The natural environment can give a unique sense of exhilaration and challenge. • Overcoming challenge builds the character and gives an opportunity for personal development and self-discovery.	• The natural environment can be dangerous. • Weather conditions can change rapidly and there can be unpredictable occurrences, for example, flash floods. • Real risk must be avoided at all costs (see p. 98–99 under outdoor education in Chapter 10), whereas situations that feel risky (but are in fact safe) give a sense of adventure and excitement.

Functional

Sportsmanship

Fair play

Physical prowess

Physical endeavour

Dysfunctional

Gamesmanship

3 Sport

On the **functional** (positive) side, sport is:

- a highly competitive, highly organized and structured activity requiring a high level of commitment and skill.
- a unique situation in which individuals can learn and show **sportsmanship** and **fair play** (a positive moral code).
- an opportunity to show **physical prowess** (skilfulness) and **physical endeavour** (effort).
- a place to excel, make lifelong friends and become a positive role model.

Be sure that you understand the difference between sportsmanship and gamesmanship and can identify how each might affect a sporting situation.

On the **dysfunctional** (negative) side, sport might sometimes be described as:

- 'War minus the shooting' (George Orwell).
- a global opportunity for violence, deviance and hatred.
- the venue for cheating and **gamesmanship** (trying to get an unfair advantage without actually breaking the letter of the law).

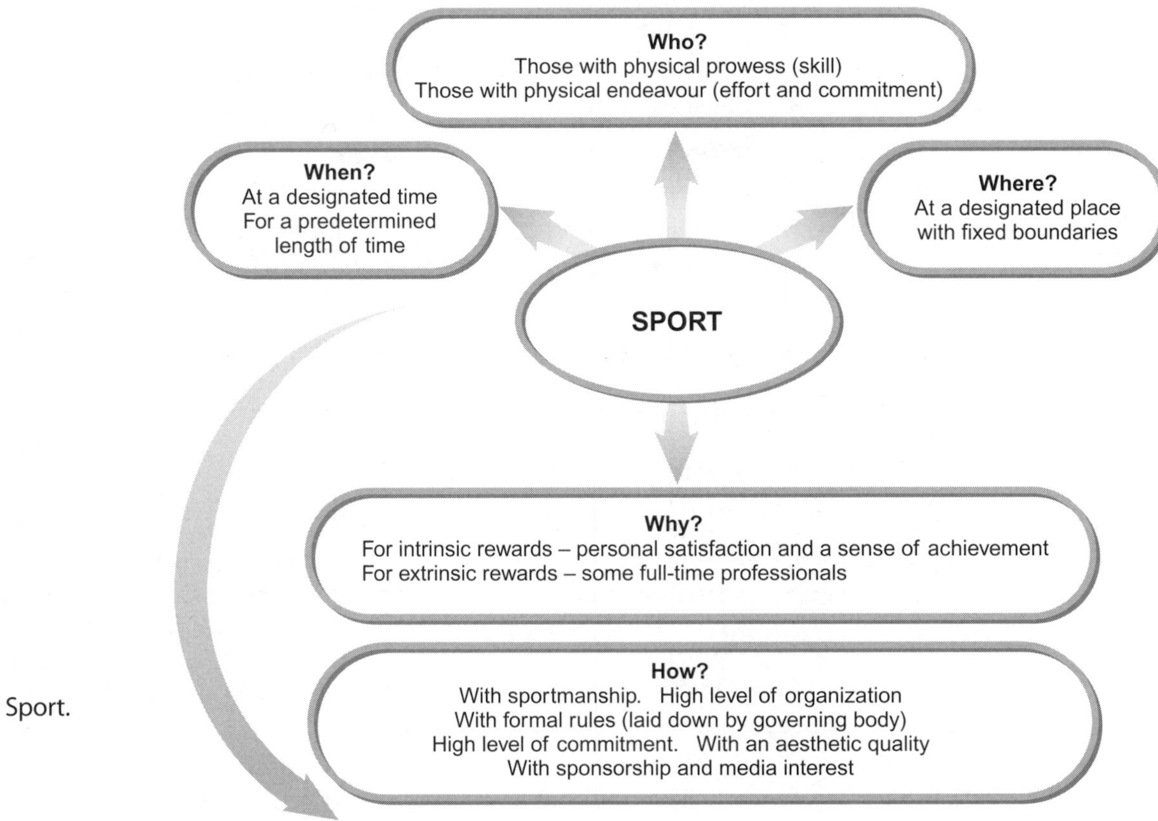

Fig. 11.02 Sport.

For further information on what makes a sport, see pp. 192–7 in *Advanced PE for OCR, AS.*

What makes a sport a sport?

The more often that the following features fit a particular activity, the more likely it is that the activity could be classified as sport.

1 Tradition – is the activity traditionally called a sport?

2 Physical exertion – does the activity involve strenuous movement?

3 Competition – does the activity involve competition against oneself or others?

4 Rules – is there a National Governing Body for the administration and rule making of the activity?

5 Behaviour – do performers in the activity usually show commitment, skill and fair play?

The same activity can be pursued as physical recreation or as sport.

Physical recreation	Sport
Jogging	Running/athletics
Paddling	Swimming or canoeing
A 'knock around'	A tennis match
A 'kick-about'	A football match
Pony trekking	Three day eventing

HOT TIPS

Remember there are few definites in our field of study and this can lead to heated discussion. Make sure you argue your point with characteristics and key words.

What is the difference between the activities listed in the two columns of the table?

- Level of competition
- Level of skill
- Level of commitment
- Level of adherence to National Governing Body rules
- Level of media coverage and sponsorship
- The quality of the venue
- The stringency of start and finish times.

KEY WORDS

Amateur

Professional

Amateurism and professionalism

- **Amateur** is from the Latin word *amare* – to love. To take part in sport as an amateur is to take part for pleasure, not for financial gain.
- A **professional** is someone who takes part for payment – it is their job.

Originally, amateur and professional status was determined by social class.

HOT TIPS

Always do what the question asks you to do. It may simply ask you to identify different characteristics of sport or it could ask you to compare physical recreation with sport. Check the command words – identify, compare, contrast.

Does Britain still have an amateur approach to sport?

- Central government shows less commitment and involvement than some other countries.
- Central government gives limited financial support to sport.
- Not all outstanding performers get lottery funding.
- Facilities are inferior to many other countries.
- Many coaches are still unpaid amateurs.
- Time for PE in schools is limited.
- Primary schools seldom have PE specialists.
- The majority of sports clubs in the UK are voluntary and run by unpaid amateurs.
- National Governing Bodies of sport still rely on volunteer administrators.

HOT TIPS

Historically it was class not payment that determined one's status as amateur or professional. 'Professional' does not just mean that you excel in sport – it means that you get paid.

Sport for all and elite sport

The term 'sport for all' implies that everyone has (or should have) the opportunity to take part in the sport of their choice, irrespective of their skill level, commitment or any social or cultural differences such as wealth, gender or age.

Elite sport refers to the very best performers being given the necessary support in order to achieve international success.

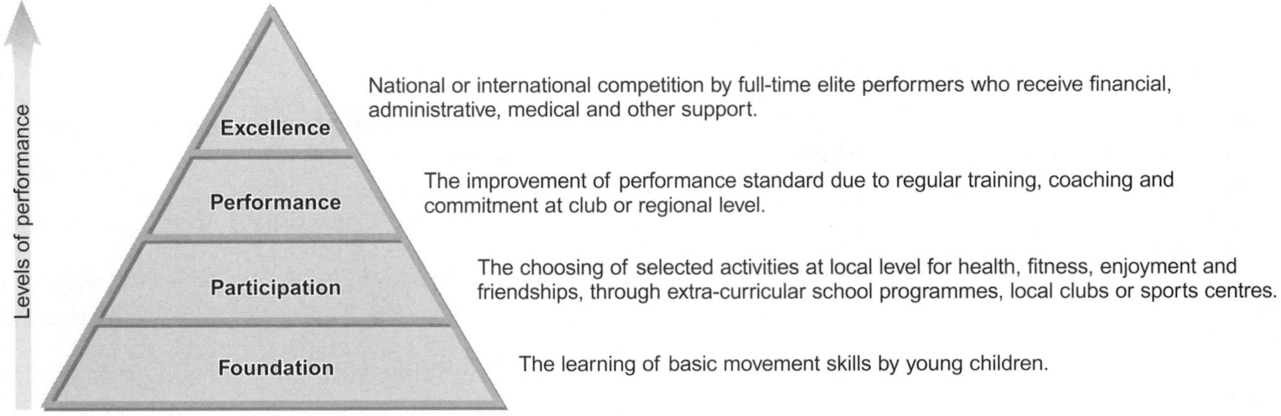

Fig. 11.03 The performance pyramid.

HOT TIPS

In an exam, you could be asked to simply name or to name and explain each level of the performance pyramid

The performance pyramid represents both sport for all (mass participation) and elite sport (sporting excellence).

4 The role of the coach

Coaches adopt many different roles (or wear many 'hats') in the course of their work. They are a Manager, Friend, Publicity agent, Administrator, First aider, Motivator and Disciplinarian to name just a few.

There are three central roles of the coach.

Instructor	Trainer	Educator
• Gives instructions – often about rules of safety. • One-way communication. No feedback from learner.	• Interested in outcome or performance. • Gives advice on technique, training, and so on. • Two-way communication increases as skill of performer increases.	• Interested in the whole person as an individual. • Concerned with experience as much as the outcome. • A two-way relationship.

HOT TIPS

Remember that the instructor, trainer and educator are the same person – they just take on the most appropriate role (wear the most suitable 'hat') for each situation.

Make sure you are able to give examples of the different roles in a practical situation. How/when would the coach be a motivator, disciplinarian or friend?

CHECK !

Go back to the overview diagrams on pp. 93 and 104. If you are satisfied with your knowledge and understanding, tick off the sections that you have revised so far. If you are not satisfied, then revisit those sections and refer to the pages in the 'Need to know more?'

For further information on the role of the coach, see pp. 197–9 in *Advanced PE for OCR, AS.*

Exam practice

1 Identify key characteristics of sport. (4 marks)

2 Contrast playing tennis as physical recreation with playing tennis as a sport. (3 marks)

3 Argue for and against snooker being classed as a sport. (4 marks)

4 Name and explain **three** of the four levels of the performance pyramid. (6 marks)

5 The roles of a sports coach are many and varied. Using practical examples from a sport of your choice, explain the roles of instructor, trainer and educator. (3 marks)

Now go to p. 163 to check your answers.!

Chapter 12 **Sport and culture**

Chapter overview

Chapter 12: Sport and culture

1 Survival of traditional sports and festivals in Britain	☐
2 Tribal societies	☐
3 Emergent societies	☐
4 The links between sport and commercialism, and sport and politics	☐

NEED TO KNOW MORE?

For further information on sport and culture, see pp. 200–18 in *Advanced PE for OCR, AS*.

Tick the box when you are satisfied with your level of knowledge and understanding for each topic within this chapter.

KEY WORDS

Culture

Society

Sport and culture

Sport and culture

- Sport reflects the **culture** (traditions, customs, sports, pastimes) and **society** (interacting community) in which it exists.
- '**Sport and culture**' is the link between culture and the physical activities within it.

1 Survival of traditional sports and festivals in Britain

Surviving traditional sports and festivals are either single sport occasions (for example, the Ashbourne football match) or multi-sport festivals (for example, the Highland Games).

On Shrove Tuesday 2003, Prince Charles started the annual two-day Ashbourne football match praising the

> great Derbyshire and Ashbourne tradition . . . which takes place on roads, in the car parks, and any available open space in the town apart from the crematorium.

Fig. 12.01 The Prince of Wales before the start of the traditional Shrove Tuesday Ashbourne Game.

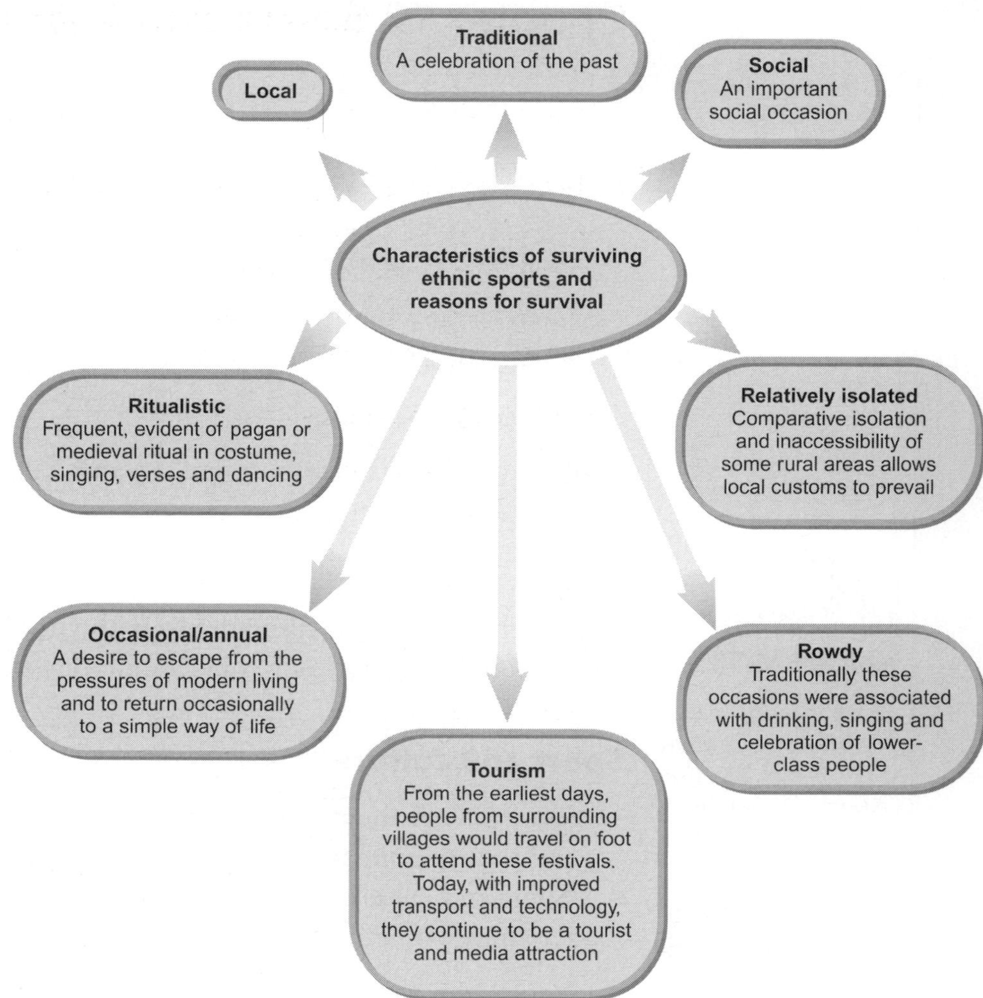

Fig. 12.02 Characteristics of surviving ethnic sports and reasons for survival.

2 Tribal societies

Tribal societies were affected by **colonialization** – the nineteenth-century Empire-building by dominant nations who took over and governed previously independent regions of the world.

Phases of development

Colonialization

Ethnic identity

- Pre-colonial – the inherent activities of a society before the arrival and influence of British and other colonialists.
- Colonial – changes brought about by the imposition of foreign customs and behaviour.
- Post-colonial – the contemporary scene with possible re-emergence of traditional **ethnic identity** (the unique behaviour and characteristics of the community, which are often based on tradition and ritual).

Spread of Imperialism and team games around the world

During the reign of Queen Victoria (1837–1901):

- British life became more civilized and technologically advanced.
- English public schools became hotbeds of team games for the development of manly qualities and character.
- Missionaries took Christianity far afield.
- Britain gathered and colonized a vast empire.

Case study of rugby in Samoa

Samoa is on the equator in the south-western Pacific. It was discovered in 1722 and explored from 1830.

Pre-colonial

In pre-colonial Samoa sports and pastimes:

- used the natural environment
- were for small groups or whole villages, sometimes against another village or district
- were great social occasions
- were pursued for village not individual success and glory.

Colonial

- Team games such as cricket and rugby were introduced by those who colonized the island.
- Rugby appealed to the lifestyle, temperament, flair and physique of the Samoans.

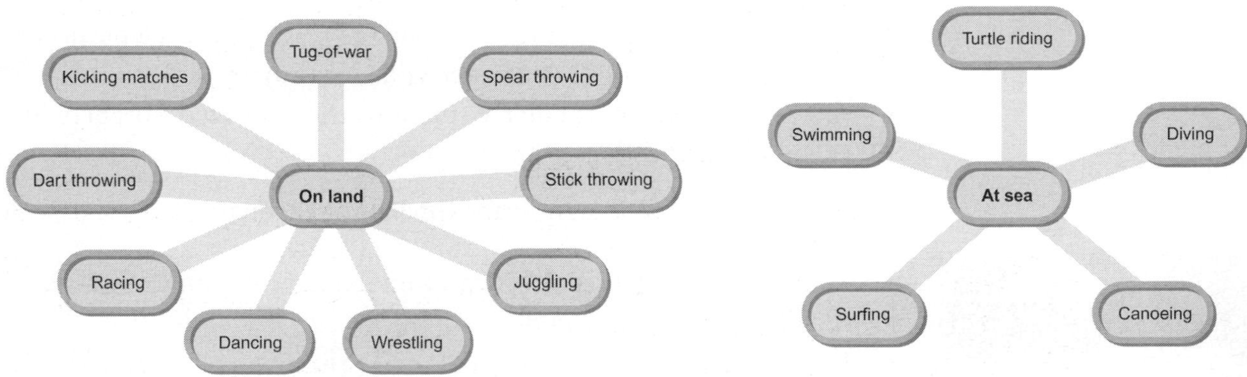

Fig. 12.03 Sports and pastimes in Pre-Colonial Samoa.

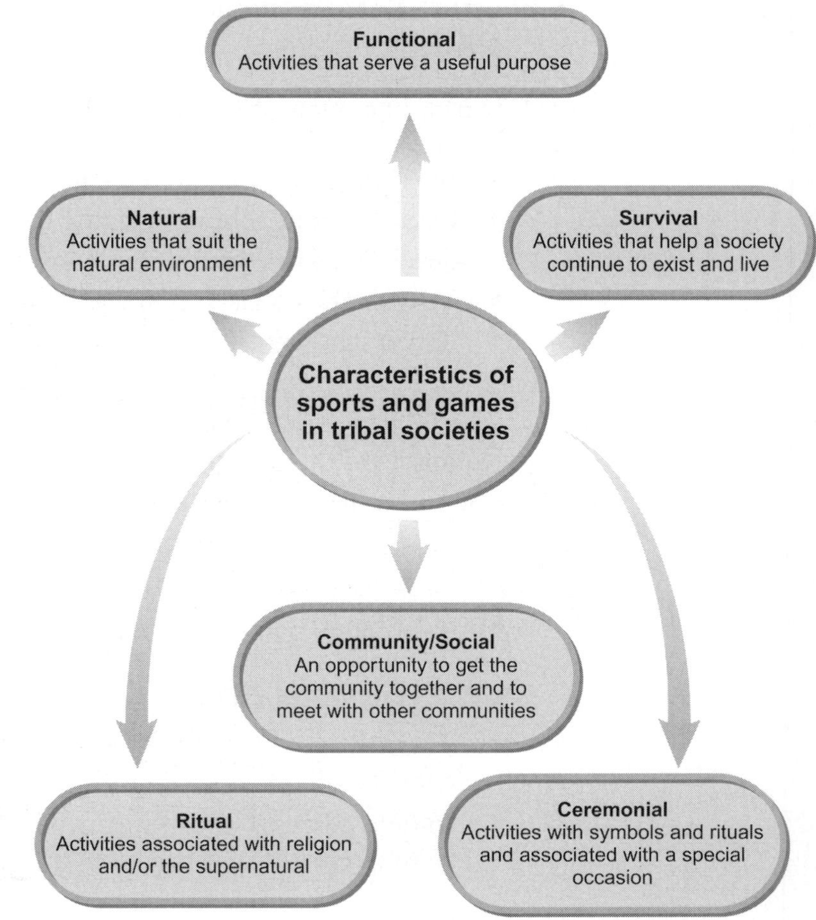

HOT TIPS

Make sure that you understand the meaning of each of the characteristics of sport in tribal cultures.

Fig. 12.04 Sports and games in tribal societies.

Post-colonial

Rugby had an important place in post-colonial Samoa because:

- it unified villages as the old sports had done
- it was an ideal medium for inter-village rivalry and celebration
- it took the place of violent inter-village combats
- the 7s game was particularly suited to the restricted numbers in each village and flair of the players.

The Samoan 'Haka' is significant for many reasons.

Fig. 12.05 The Samoan 'Haka'.

- It shows a re-emergence of traditional Samoan ethnic identity.
- It calls upon the war gods.
- It acts as a link between pre-colonial primitive pastimes and modern sport.
- It unites the players with each other.
- It unites the players with all the inhabitants of Samoa.
- It psyches out the opposition.

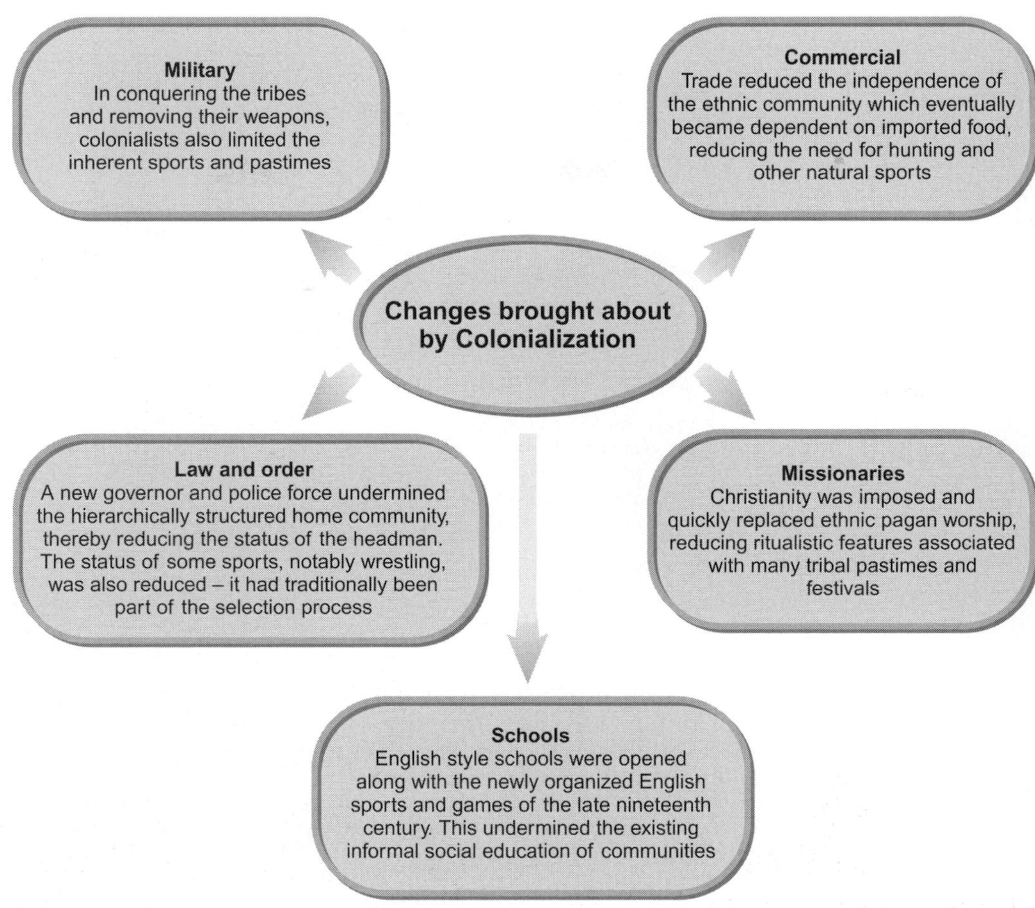

Fig. 12.06 The impact of colonialization.

3 Emergent societies

- Emergent countries are less economically developed countries, for example, some in Africa, the Far East and Central and South America.
- They are emerging (or developing) from tribal origins to greater political stability and socio-economic and technological levels.
- Emergent societies sometimes use sport as a vehicle for advancement.

Case study of distance running in Kenya

- Settlers from other countries have influenced Kenya.
- Before colonialization, the inherent physical activities in Kenya were tribal in nature and they included dancing and fighting games.
- Kenya gained independence in 1963.

- Kenya competed for the first time as an independent nation in the 1968 Mexico Olympics, winning nine medals in middle and long distance running events.

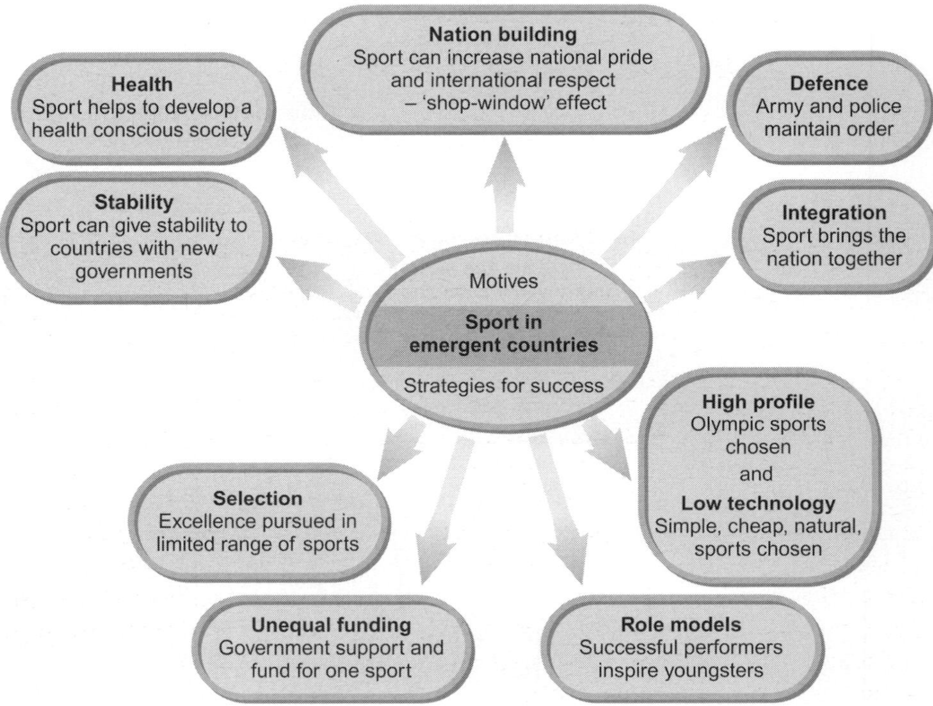

Fig. 12.07 Sport in emergent countries: motives and strategies for success.

Reasons for Kenya's running success

- High altitude training, which helps oxygen efficiency.
- Running is part of their natural lifestyle.
- The physique of the Kenyans suits the event.
- Kenyans have a well-balanced high-quality protein and high carbohydrate diet.
- Athletes receive expert coaching (initially it was from foreign coaches).
- In common with all successful elite performers, Kenyan athletes show immense dedication and commitment.

4 The links between sport and commercialism, and sport and politics

- International sporting success increases a country's status.
- Advanced societies use sport to show their supposed superiority over other nations.

Capitalist economies

Socialist economies

Mixed economies

Democracy

Win ethic

Capitalist economies are those where private ownership dominates and is encouraged. In capitalist economies, private wealth is used to produce and distribute goods and services. In **socialist economies,** state ownership dominates and controls commerce, policy and practice. In **mixed economies,** both private and public enterprise operates together. A **democracy** is a country where the people have the right to participate in public affairs.

Sport and commercialism – the 'American Dream'	Sport and politics – the 'Shop Window'
• In the USA, sport is big business. • Professional sport is inextricably linked with sponsorship and the media. • Private and corporate businesses use sport to promote products and to achieve goodwill. • High school sport has a high profile and attracts huge sponsorship with the best high school 'athletes' gaining scholarships to colleges and universities. • College players are almost 'professionals' in terms of dedication, support and pressure, and the best are 'drafted' into professional sport. • The '**win ethic**' dominates (winning is the only thing that matters) with professional sport reflecting the competitive and capitalist nature of US society.	• In China for example, sport is used as a political tool. • Sport and politics are inextricably linked. • Politicians use sport to promote their country and their political system, though sport can also be used for internal motives. • The Olympic Games is used as the 'stage'. • Potentially successful athletes are sought and given all possible support in order to gain success. • They can also be abused in terms of pressure (possibly to take drugs) and other forms of abuse.

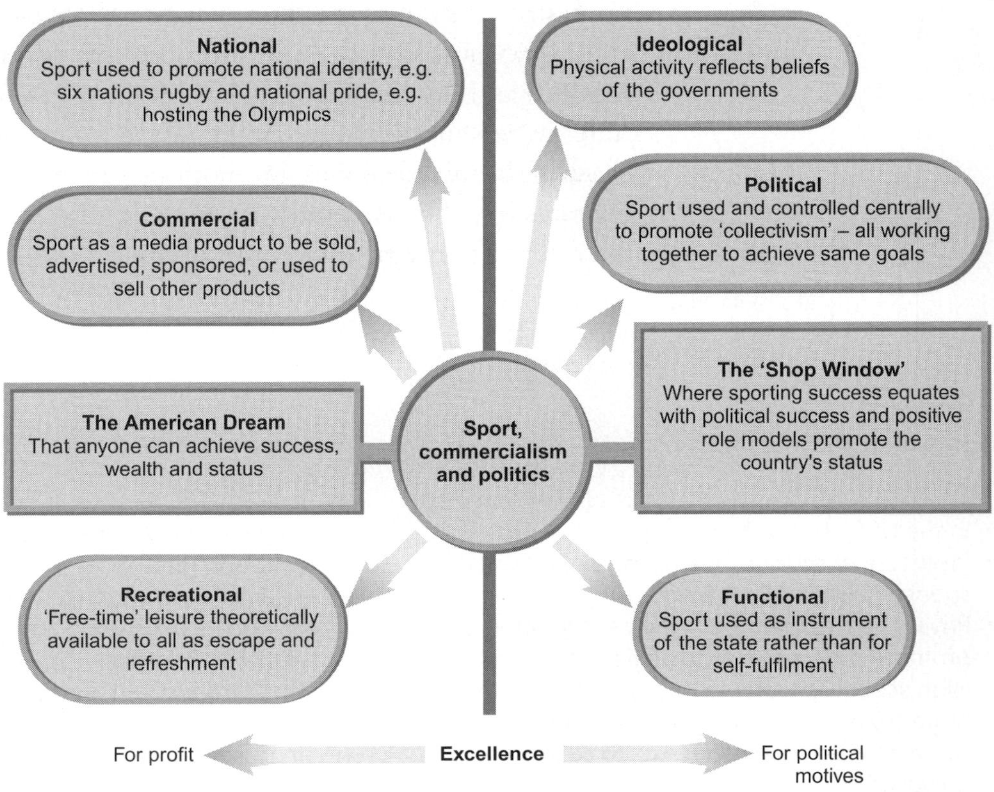

Fig. 12.08 Commercial and political approaches to sport.

Make sure that you know how commercialism and politics can both drive countries.

CHECK !

Go back to the overview diagrams on pp. 93 and 111. If you are satisfied with your knowledge and understanding, tick off the sections that you have revised so far. If you are not satisfied, then revisit those sections and refer to the pages in the 'Need to know more?'

Exam practice

1 Identify **two** characteristics of a named ethnic sport that still occurs in the UK today and give reasons for its survival. (6 marks)

2 Many tribal countries were colonized by outsiders in the eighteenth century. Identify and explain two changes brought about by colonialization. (4 marks)

3 Emergent societies sometimes use sport as a vehicle for advancement. Why do emergent countries seek sporting success and how do they achieve it? (6 marks)

4 Some countries use sport for political reasons. State possible positive **and** negative effects of sport being used for political reasons. (4 marks)

Now go to p. 165 to check your answers.

Chapter 13 **Sporting issues analysis**

Chapter overview

Chapter 13: Sporting issues analysis

1 What is sporting excellence? ☐
2 Structure and organization of sport in the UK ☐
3 Funding for sport ☐
4 Influence of the media ☐
5 Influence of sponsorship ☐
6 Ethics and high-level sport ☐
7 Drugs and sport ☐
8 Sport and mass participation ☐
9 Discrimination in sport ☐

For further information on sporting issues analysis, see pp. 219–63 in *Advanced PE for OCR, AS*.

Tick the box when you are satisfied with your level of knowledge and understanding for each topic within this chapter.

1 What is sporting excellence?

Figure 13.01 (see page 121) shows how the main themes of excellence and mass participation link with other sporting issues.

Sporting excellence Key terms	Mass participation Key terms
Policy – government initiatives and government support including policy on funding. Policy is based on ideology (a particular system of ideas, beliefs and values).	**Opportunity** – features that exist to increase the chance to participate, for example, availability of time, social or physical access, appropriate playing standard, suitable cost, and so on.

Provision – features that encourage or allow excellence or participation, for example, the availability of suitable facilities, equipment, coaches, competition, courses, and so on.

Administration – the structure, organization and funding of sport by organizations (see Figure 13.02).	**Esteem** – self-confidence and respect from others. Linked to societal status.

There are regular examination questions on initiatives for increasing excellence in the UK. These can include:

- UKSI network of centres and Centres of Excellence
- National Lottery money and the World Class Performance programme
- specialist sports colleges with their potentially high levels of coaching and facilities
- the work of the Youth Sport Trust
- coach development and work of sports coach UK
- attracting world-class events
- building the base of the performance pyramid with initiatives such as:
  - PE initiatives, for example, sportsmark and Active Schools
  - the TOP programmes
  - work of School Sports Co-ordinators in schools and Sports Development Officers in the community
  - the Active Communities Development Fund (for target groups)
  - Sport Action Zones
  - Active Sports programme (which targets nine sports)
  - Sportsearch
  - the work of sports colleges to encourage participation.

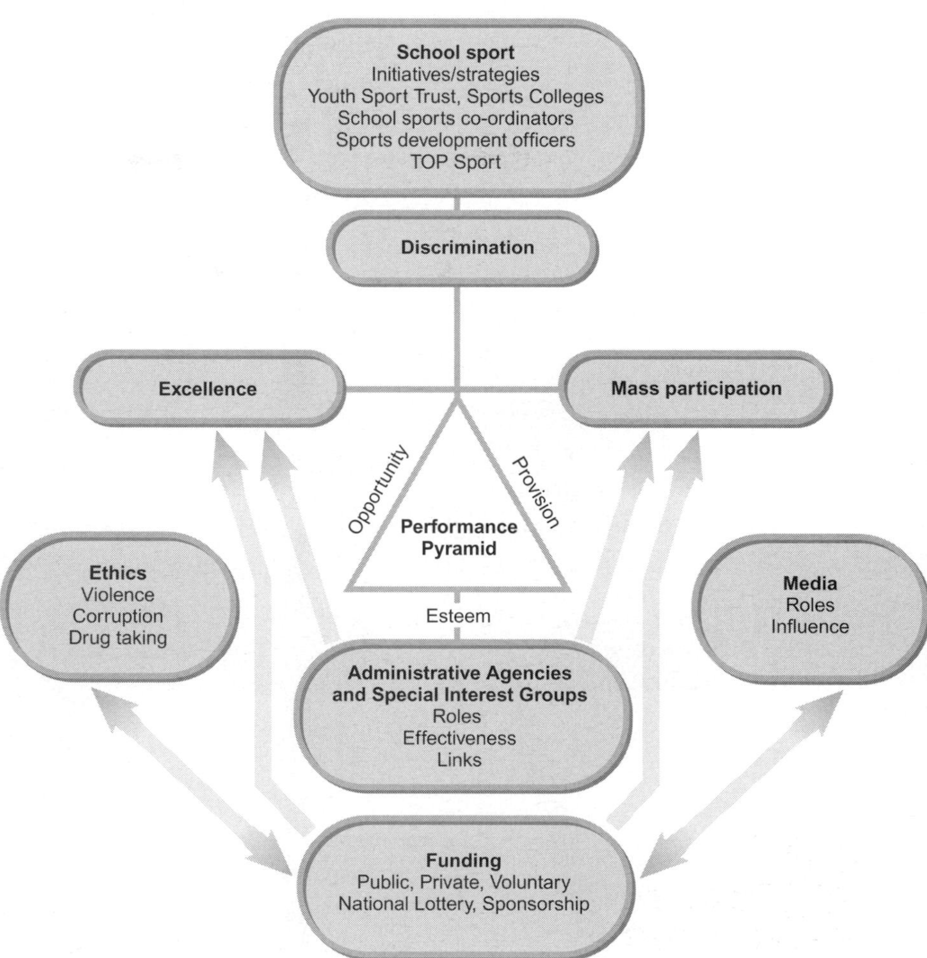

Fig. 13.01 Sporting issues.

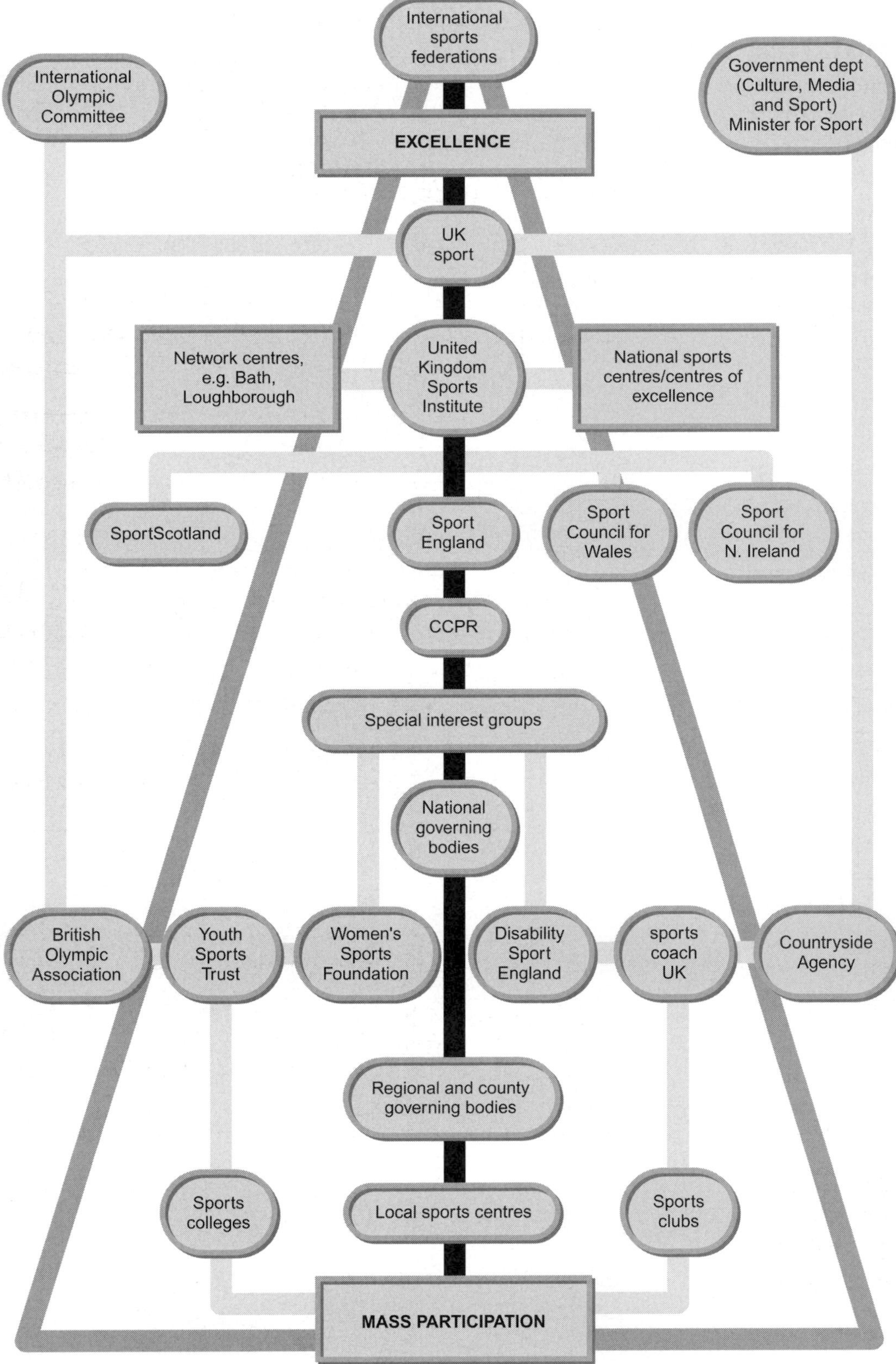

Fig. 13.02 Organizations influencing mass participation and sporting excellence in the UK.

2 Structure and organization of sport in the UK

The UK has a decentralised system where power and control are locally held by individual co-ordinating organizations.

You need to know and understand what the different organizations do to promote sport for the masses and/or for the elite in the UK.

Name UK Sport

Overall aim To develop elite sport in UK

. . . and for excellence

- Oversees UK Sports Institute (UKSI)
- Involved in 'More Medals' aspect of World Class Performance programme
- Runs doping control
- Distributes lottery funding
- Attracts major sporting events

Name UK Sports Institute (UKSI) and Home Country institutes

Overall aim To provide Britain's best performers with the facilities and support services they need to compete and win at the highest level

. . . and for excellence

- Provides the High Performance Coaching programme (developed by BOA and sports coach UK) to develop elite coaches
- Provides the Athlete Career and Education (ACE UK) programme to improve an elite athlete's sporting performance and personal development through an individualized career and education programme
- Works, where possible and appropriate, with gifted and talented performers from local Sports Colleges

Name Home country organizations, for example, Sport England

Overall aim 'Making England an active and successful sporting nation.'

Sport England wants more:

- opportunities to play sport – and participation
- people to stay in sport – through an effective network of clubs, sports facilities, coaches, volunteers and competitive opportunities
- opportunities to achieve success in sport.

Sport England's previous motto was 'More people, more places and more medals'

. . . and for excellence	The World Class Performance programme (delivered by both UK Sport and Sport England) directs money to the country's top performers
. . . and mass participation	• The Active Communities Development Fund targets ethnic communities, people with disabilities, women and girls, and people on low incomes. • Deprived areas can be targeted as 'Sport Action Zones' with facility development and regeneration a priority. • The Active Sports programme gets lottery funding for facilities and equipment for nine targeted sports (including Rugby Union, athletics and basketball). • The School Sport Co-ordinator programme aims to increase sports opportunities for young people through co-ordinated PE, school sport and out of school learning activities.

Name	**National Governing Bodies (for example, UK Athletics)**
Overall aim	• To maintain rules and regulations • To control finances • To plan and implement education programmes for coaches and officials • To appoint technical directors to deliver against performance plans
. . . and for excellence	• To select performers for World Class Funding • To select and prepare national squads • To deal with disciplinary welfare issues • To organize national competition • To co-ordinate with International Governing Body
. . . and mass participation	• To encourage participation at all levels • To organize local competitions • To plan and co-ordinate support programmes for affiliated clubs

Special interest groups

Name Women's Sports Foundation (WSF)

Overall aim	To improve and promote opportunities for women and girls in sport at every level by influencing changes in sports policy, practice and culture
. . . and for excellence	Raises the profile of British sportswomen by working closely with the media and other organizations
. . . and mass participation	• Promotes the benefits of an active lifestyle • Campaigns for changes in policy to increase opportunity • Creates and promotes models of best practice

REGISTERED CHARITY NUMBER 297035

Name Disability Sport England (DSE)

Overall aim	To improve awareness of and image of disability sport
. . . and for excellence	• Works with other organizations to identify talent • Has a national scouting programme • Has national championships for specific sports
. . . and mass participation	• To provide opportunities for disabled people to participate in sport • To promote the benefits of sport and physical recreation by disabled people • To enhance the image, awareness and understanding of disability sport • To encourage disabled people to play an active role in the development of their sport

Name sports coach UK

Overall aim	To develop a coaching system that supports and enhances sports coaches and coaching throughout the UK
. . . and for excellence	• To develop high level coaches • To develop sports research projects
. . . and mass participation	• Has coaching award structure • Supports new coaches with courses, resources and study packs • Co-ordinates the Coaching for Teachers initiative, which aims to improve coaching standards within schools

3 Funding for sport

Providing for mass participation and international sporting success is very expensive.

Funding for sport in this country can be divided into the following sectors:

- public – from central government and local authorities
- private – from companies whose aim is to make money, but who also wish to support sport
- voluntary – from National Governing Bodies and local private sports clubs, which exist for their members.

There are other specific funding schemes, such as Sportsmatch, which is the government's grass roots sports sponsorship incentive scheme. It is funded by the Department for Culture, Media and Sport through grant aid from Sport England and administered in England by the Institute of Sports Sponsorship. Sportsmatch can match pound for pound commercial business sponsorship for a grass roots sporting event or activity.

Fig. 13.03 Sportsmatch.

HOT TIPS

Note that there are funding concerns in British sport.

- Money from the exchequer (government) is comparatively low.
- Pressure on lottery funding keeps increasing.
- Many sports halls and centres were built in the 1970s and need millions spent on them to bring them up to date.
- The number of lottery tickets being sold has reduced so the amount of money available from the lottery is potentially lower.

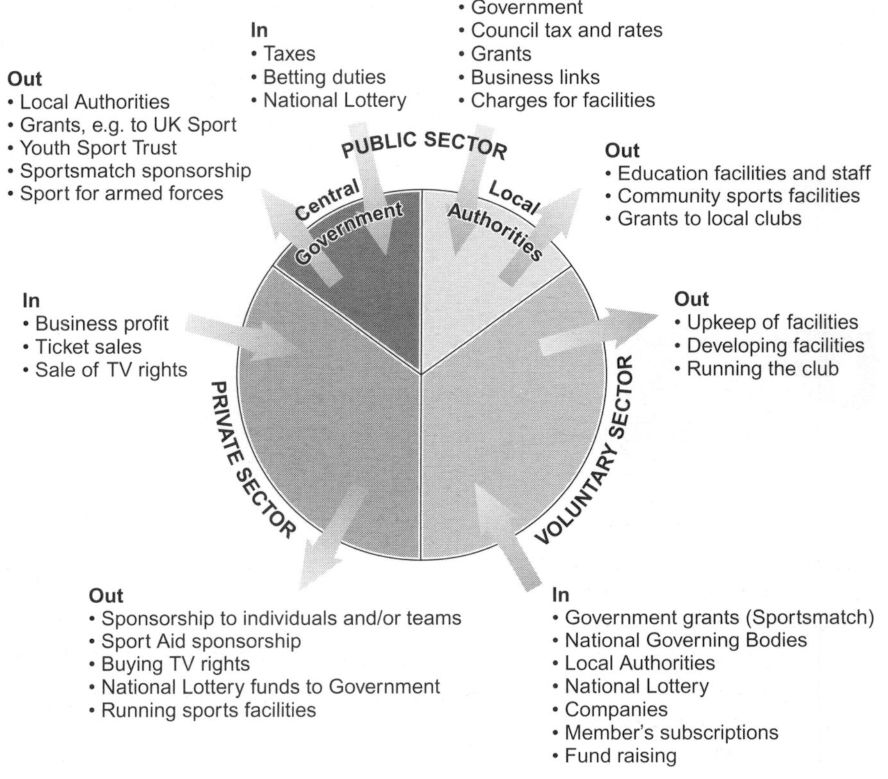

Fig. 13.04 The funding pie is made up of public, private and voluntary sectors.

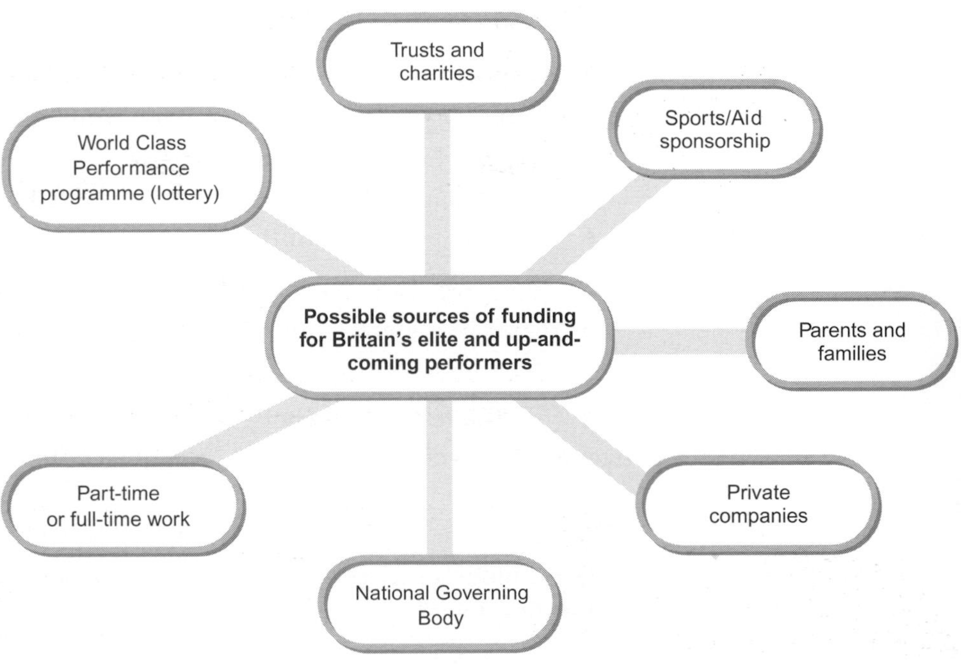

Fig. 13.05 Possible sources of funding for Britain's elite and up-and-coming performers.

The media is made up of TV, radio, newspapers, magazines, the Internet, books, films and videos. It heavily invests in and powerfully influences sport. It can affect sporting participation (both positively and negatively) and encourage sporting excellence. Sport and the media (and therefore also sponsorship which is fuelled by the media) are inextricably linked.

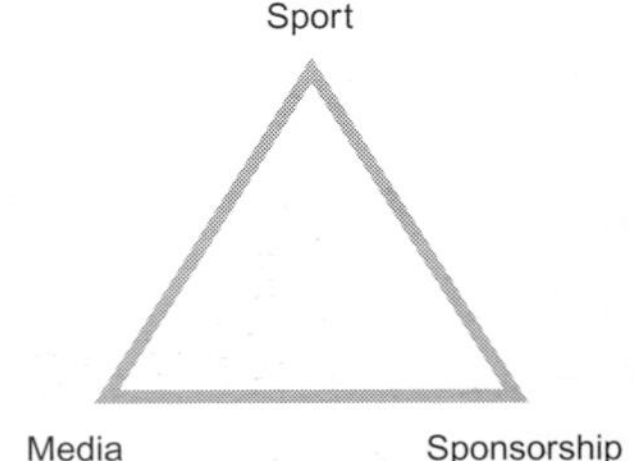

Fig. 13.06 The 'golden triangle' or inter-relationship between sport, sponsorship and the media.

4 Influence of the media

The media has four key roles.

1 To inform, for example, on results, team analysis or player preparation, or behaviour.

2 To educate, for example, on global sporting issues, sport skills, coaching techniques or local sporting provision.

3 To entertain, for example, with live coverage of an event or information about stars' private lives, or a documentary on a particular team's pre-competition preparation.

4 To advertise either directly or indirectly through sponsorship.

HOT TIPS

Remember that any media feature can have elements of each of the four key roles or one role may dominate. Try to have examples of TV programmes or articles that predominantly either inform, educate, entertain or advertise.

Points to consider when studying the media

- Is sport now simply a branch of the advertising industry?
- Can sport retain its traditional nature and values *and* benefit from the money offered by the media?
- Has money corrupted sport or saved it from economic disaster?
- Has the need to win for money led to corruption and cheating?

The relationship between sport and the media

Positive outcomes: the media can . . .	Negative outcomes: the media can . . .
Shatter stereotypes	Create and reinforce stereotypes
Produce positive role models and sports stars who become media stars	Invade the privacy of sports personalities and require them to perform more frequently than is physically or mentally desirable
Bring sport to millions	Overload people with too much sport or too much of a specific sport
Give exposure to minority sports	Concentrate on mainstream male dominated team sports
Inspire participation	Encourage passive spectatorism
Inform, educate and entertain	Concentrate on the dramatic, spectacular or trivial, for example, violence, or trivial aspects of women's sport, which gives an unrealistic or damaging image to the sport
Influence rule changes which encourage creativity and attacking play	Influence rule changes which are not in the interests of the game or the players
Influence prime time screening of big events for our entertainment	Influence coverage of events at times that are unhelpful to participants
Encourage international friendship and acceptance	Heighten national prejudice

Make sure that you can comment on both positive and negative influences of the media on sport.

Sponsorship

Institute of Sports Sponsorship (ISS)

5 Influence of sponsorship

- Sports **sponsorship** is the provision of money (or other support) to gain recognition and increased income.
- Sponsorship agencies bring sponsors and sports bodies together to organize events or programmes.
- Companies invest in perimeter advertising around and on pitches.
- Agents promote particular competitors for mutual financial benefit.
- Performers endorse (give their backing) to products by displaying the company name on their clothing or equipment.

- Sports stars use their celebrity status to advertise away from the sports arena.
- Sponsorship is uneven across sports.
- Minority sports or those pursued by minority groups find it hard to get sponsorship because of limited media coverage.
- The **Institute of Sports Sponsorship** is a national non-profit making organization made up of companies that sponsor sport. The ISS aims to protect the traditional nature of sport, help companies to get fair returns on outlay, co-operate with other organizations and runs the Sportsmatch scheme (see p. 126).

Sponsorship has advantages and disadvantages to both performers and sponsors.

The performer	
Advantages of sponsorship	**Disadvantages of sponsorship**
Full-time training possible because sponsor meets expenses	Performers can become too reliant on a particular sponsor
Financial security after retirement can be provided	It can be limited or withdrawn, which does not provide security
Full concentration on sport possible	Some sponsorship gives a bad image to sport, for example, alcohol
	Performers, teams and events can be manipulated or exploited to suit the sponsor
	Generous sponsorship only available to the few
The sponsor	
Advantages of sponsorship	**Disadvantages of sponsorship**
Healthy, positive image forged	If performer behaves badly, it can reflect on the sponsor
Tax bill reduced	It is an uncertain investment – sporting success not guaranteed
Excellent advertising can be gained, which generates income	If the event is disrupted, media exposure is lost
Hospitality at big sporting events	
Goodwill increased	

HOT TIPS

Be able to give one or two examples of different types of sponsorship, sponsored events, leagues or teams.

6 Ethics and high-level sport

In this country, the way that games and sports were played (that is, with sportsmanship and fair play) has traditionally been as important as the result. By the late twentieth century, however, there had been a move towards the American 'win at all costs' ethic and the 'amateur' attitudes had all but disappeared from professional sport. The stakes

For further information on sportsmanship and gamesmanship, see p. 196 in *Advanced PE for OCR, AS*.

Make sure that you understand the difference between sportsmanship and gamesmanship and can identify how each might affect a sporting situation.

The stakes and prize money increased, the outcome became imperative, the pressure intensified and gamesmanship (the stretching of rules to the limit in order to gain an advantage) became more commonplace.

Violence by performers

Violence in sport seems to be a frequent occurrence. Violence by sports performers can be analysed in terms of:

- cheating – it is against the rules
- health – it can cause injury
- legality – outbursts of physical violence are increasingly countered with legal action
- role modelling – and the responsibility of high profile performers.

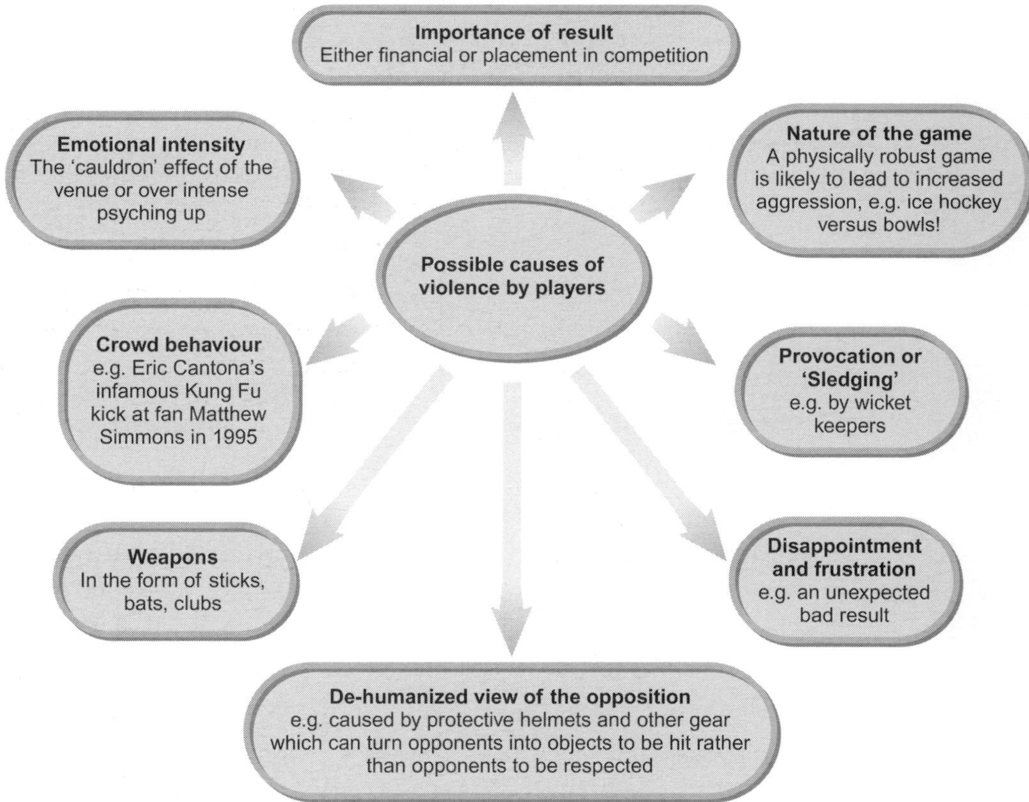

Fig. 13.07 The possible causes of violence by players.

Possible solutions to the problem of violence by players

- **Rule changes** – to combat ways that players and coaches find to dodge rules, for example changes to goalkeeping and offside rules in soccer; line out, scrummaging, kicking for touch and offside rules in Rugby Union

- **More severe penalties** – for example penalty tries, sin bins, yellow/red cards and sending off for intentional fouls on players in clear goal scoring positions
- **Education** – the CCPR, Sports Coach UK and UK Sport have produced guidelines to instil an ethos of fair play into sports performers
- **Greater numbers** – and more authority for referees, umpires and lines people
- **Technology –** video playbacks to assess and adjudicate on unfair play

Violence by spectators

Violence by spectators at sporting events is an important sociological issue. We need to review its possible causes and outline possible solutions to the problem.

Possible causes of crowd violence

- Ritual importance of the event – for example a local derby
- Violence by players on the pitch
- Pre-match hype in newspapers, on TV or at the ground
- Controversial decisions by officials
- Chanting and abuse from rival fans
- Diminished responsibility by individuals when in a large group
- Activity by a minority of violent criminals in organized gangs and members of fascist organizations who use football as an arena for serious assault 'Hooligans at football – not football hooligans'
- Limited alternative outlets for stress in modern industrial society
- The score or result
- Clumsy and primitive strategies for crowd control which incite frustration and trouble
- Religion, for example Celtic v Rangers
- Alcohol

Possible solutions to the problem of crowd violence

- Promotion of football as family entertainment
- Removal of terraces/all-seater stadiums
- CCTV around stadiums and security checks
- Tougher deterrents
- Separation of fans from different clubs
- Liaison by police in different areas of the country
- Control of alcohol
- Removal of perimeter fences between crowds and pitch

If a question asks for solutions to the problem of drugs in sport, make sure you do not simply list different types of drugs and explain what they are used for. Remember, answer the question set, not the one that you wish had been.

7 Drugs and sport

In spite of strict bans and increased testing, the problem of drugs and sport continues.

Why do performers take drugs?

Physiological reasons
To build muscle, increase energy
Increase oxygen transport
Lose weight, train harder
Mask injury and reduce tiredness

Psychological reasons
To steady nerves
To increase aggression
To increase motivation

Social reasons
Pressure to win from coaches, peers and media
By winning they can earn big money
They are prepared to 'win-at-all-costs'
Fear of not winning
Belief that everyone else is doing it!

Why shouldn't they?

Moral reasons
Gives an unfair advantage
Undermines the true spirit of sport
Reflects badly on others

Health reasons
Can be addictive, lower life expectancy and even cause death
Can lead to liver disorders and heart disease
Can suppress growth
Can cause sexual and gynaecological problems
Can affect moods and behaviour causing aggression or depression

Legal reasons
Against the law of the land
Against the laws of sport

Role modelling
Gives a bad example to others, especially young people who may copy their heroes and put their health at risk
Gives a bad image to sport and lowers its status

What is being done or could be done to solve the problem?

Stricter, more rigorous and out-of-season testing
Stricter punishments and life bans
Co-ordinated education programmes for athletes and coaches which highlight the health and moral issues surrounding drugs and sport
More money for increasingly efficient and effective testing programmes
Unified policies about the issue
Role models to reinforce their 'no drugs' position

Fig. 13.08 The issue of drugs and sport.

8 Sport and mass participation

Socio-cultural factors

Target groups

In a democracy, everyone should have the opportunity to take part in sport as regularly as they wish and at whatever level they choose in order to increase health and for general well-being. However, certain **socio-cultural factors** such as gender, age, wealth, ability or disability affect this. Sports organizations in the UK have been campaigning for 'Sport for All' for over 30 years. In Britain, certain **target groups**, such as ethnic minorities or people with disabilities, continue to be the main focus of their work.

Private and voluntary provision of facilities can be a bit confusing, especially as the voluntary sector incorporates 'private members clubs', such as local village cricket clubs. Remember though, voluntary clubs are run by volunteers who are not seeking financial gain.

Facilities for mass participation

People take part in sport at public, private and voluntary facilities.

- Public facilities – funded by local authorities for community use.
- Private facilities – privately or group owned for profit, using sport as the commodity.
- Voluntary facilities – run by and for unpaid members. They charge subscriptions to cover costs and put any profit back into the club.

9 Discrimination in sport

Discrimination

Stacking

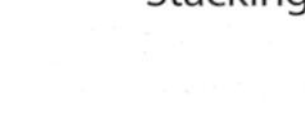

Discrimination is unfairness. If discrimination occurs in a society, it will be noticeable in the sport of that society. Discrimination is to do with:

- unfair treatment
- stereotypical images of groups of people
- an imbalance of power between groups.

Remember the work of special interest groups, such as the WSF and DSE in increasing participation by minority groups.

Some societies (for example', the USA) are stratified or layered. The dominant group are at the top while the 'newest' or least dominant group are the bottom. Layers exist in between. **Stacking** then occurs. Stacking is the disproportionate concentration of ethnic minorities in certain positions in a sports team. Stacking is mainly based on the stereotyped view that certain ethnic groups are best suited to roles requiring power and skill rather than decision-making and communication.

NEED TO KNOW MORE?

For further information on discrimination in sport, see pp 251–62 in *Advanced PE for OCR, AS*.

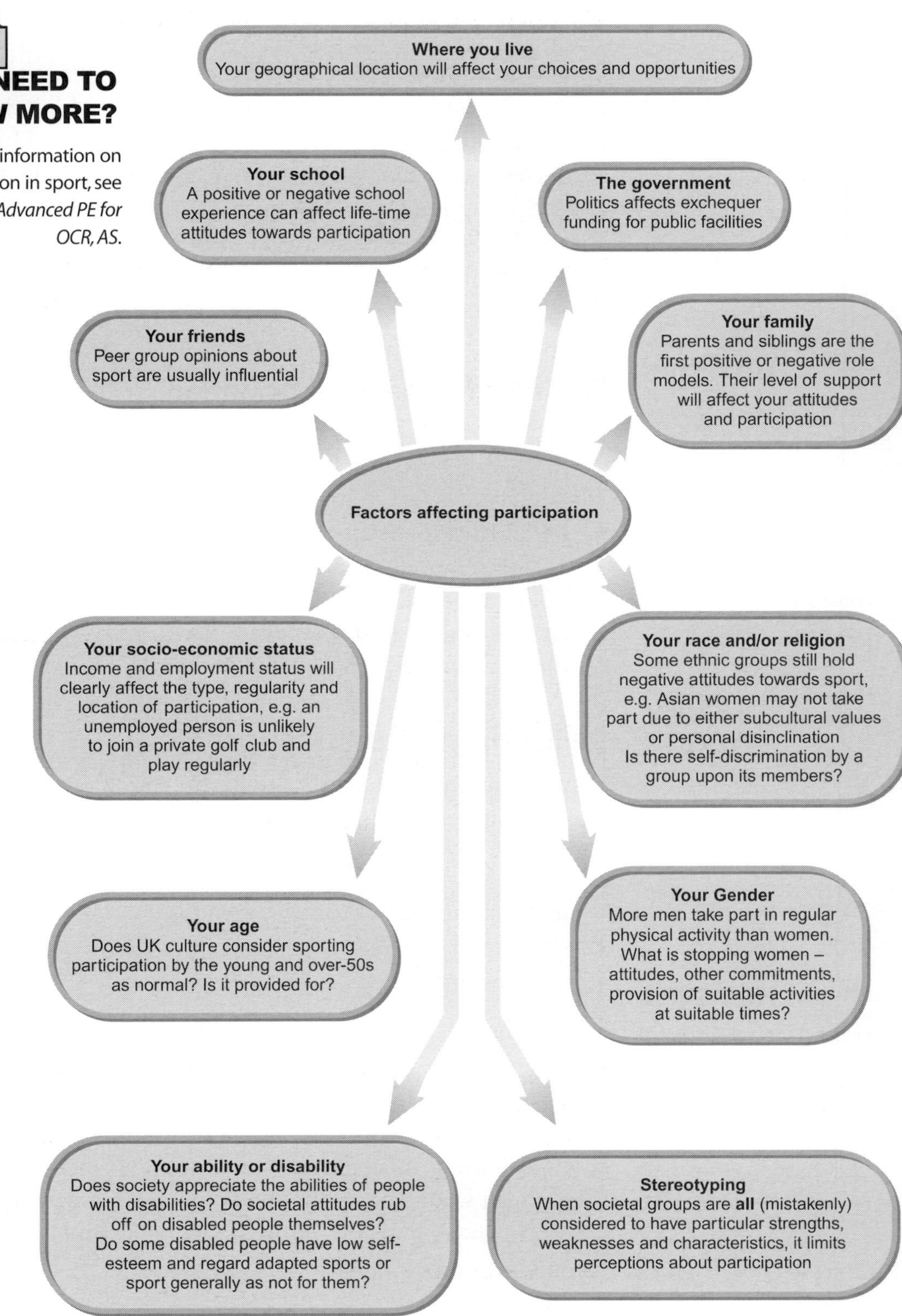

Fig. 13.09 Factors affecting participation in sport.

The following minority groups should be studied:

- people on low incomes
- women
- ethnic minorities
- people with disabilities
- the old and young.

Sport England targets deprived areas, known as 'Sport Action Zones', with facility development and regeneration a priority.

Social class/wealth

Social class refers to:

- income
- background
- societal status
- education.

Evidence shows that lower socio-economic backgrounds lead to lower sports participation. This may be due to:

- cost of participation
- lower levels of health and fitness
- low self-esteem
- lack of opportunities
- lack of role models in dominant positions
- a belief that 'sport is not for me'
- an aversion to the dominant middle-class culture surrounding sport centres.

Women

- Women were excluded from the first modern Olympic games in 1896.
- Baron Pierre de Coubertin, the founder, said, 'Women have but one task, that of crowning the winner with garlands.'
- In the Summer Olympics of 1988, there were twice as many male as female competitors.
- 92 per cent of coaches were male.

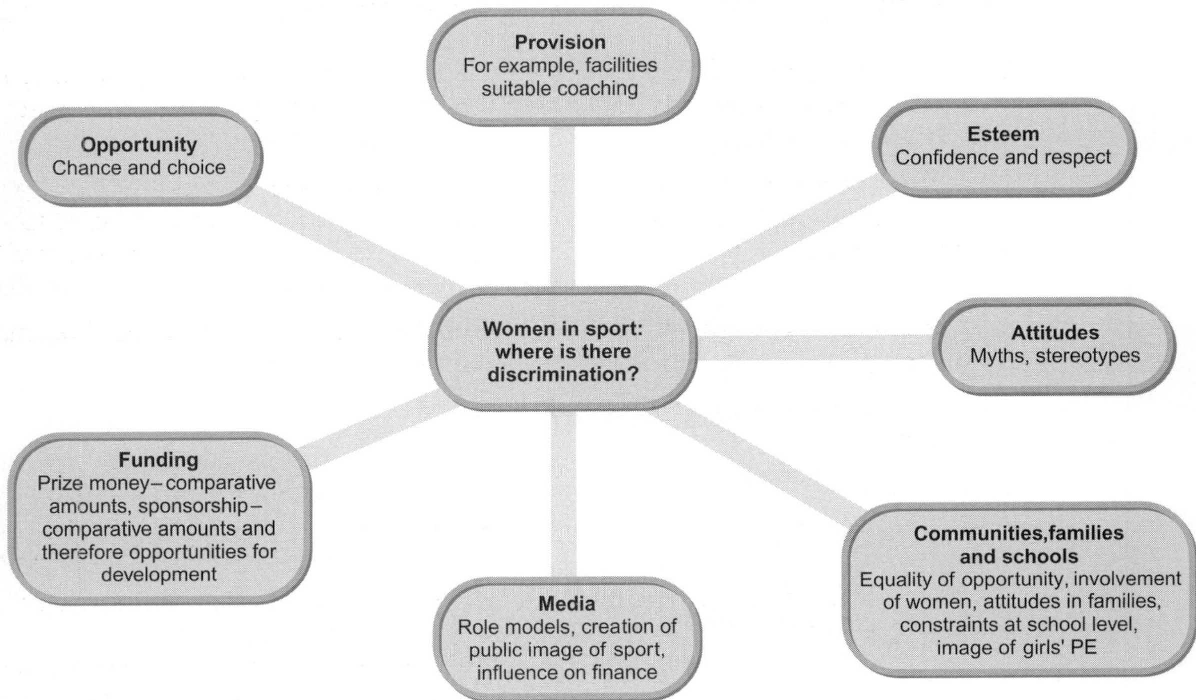

Fig. 13.10 Factors influencing participation and achievement of women and girls in sport.

Ethnic minorities

- Britain is a multi-cultural and multi-racial society.
- Racism stems from prejudice linked with the power of one racial group over another.
- Racism leads to discrimination or unfairness.
- Stereotypical thinking should be challenged through race awareness training.
- Opportunities should be provided for different cultural groups to pursue their own cultural activities.

In 1993, the then Sports Council (now UK Sport) stated its objectives in working towards the elimination of racial disadvantage and discrimination. They wanted to:

- raise awareness of racial inequality in sport
- increase sporting opportunities for black and ethnic minority people
- improve skill levels in, and positive attitudes towards, sport by black and ethnic minority people
- increase the number of black and ethnic minority decision-makers and organizers in sport
- myths should be smashed and stereotypes challenged
- role models should be given publicity and encouragement.

The situation	Considerations
Because black people are over-represented in certain sports, problems of overall lower participation are often overlooked.	Black participation is limited by stereotyping, which channels people into certain sports or positions within teams.
Over-representation of black performers in some national sports teams seem to indicate equality of opportunity.	Black athletes have been referred to as sporting 'gladiators' who have been channelled towards sport and perhaps away from other useful life experiences (Cashmore).
Black people are encouraged to make a living from sport.	Ethnic minorities need equal encouragement to participate at a recreative level.
Successful black athletes become role models.	Only a few make it to the top.
Ethnic groups are still under-represented in terms of participation.	Information and Sport Action Zones must be provided and people from ethnic minorities encouraged into leadership roles within sport.
The majority of ethnic communities use inner city, public facilities.	Many public facilities were built in the 1970s and need urgent upgrading. Sports Development Officers need to be encouraged. Special provision must be provided for certain groups, for example, Asian women.

Sport, ability and disability

> The key issue for disabled people . . . is not to mimic the non-disabled in sport, but rather to celebrate difference, acknowledge abilities in modified sports, and to recognize, on the basis of those abilities, outstanding sporting achievement.
>
> Frank Kew (1998)

Sources of discrimination for people with disabilities include:

- attitudes and assumptions
- myths and stereotyping
- inadequately designed environments (including poor toilet and changing facilities and lack of ramps, wide car-parking bays, signs in Braille, automatic doors, and so on).

What has been, is being, or could be, done to provide fairer opportunity and provision (at both mass participation and excellence levels) for people with disabilities and to increase esteem?

- Several national disability sports associations (all under the English Federation of Disability Sport) work tirelessly to improve sport for people with disabilities.

- Increased co-operation between sporting organizations.
- Integration of non-disabled and disabled people in sport.
- Emphasis on the positive images of disabled people in sport.
- Improved access to facilities.
- Improved technology for the development of specialist wheelchairs and other specialist equipment.
- Raised awareness of the abilities of specialist athletes with disabilities through the Paralympics, Commonwealth Games, and so on.
- Adaptation and modification of sports, for example, ball games with larger, smaller or brighter balls; net games with smaller areas and lower nets; team games with larger numbers, callers for direction control, and so on.
- Provision of suitable competitions/festivals for all levels of performer.
- Provision of suitable facilities at local level for participation.
- Improved funding for facilities.
- Specialist training of specialist coaches – particularly for coaches with disabilities.
- Provision of funding for elite performers.

Integration of children with disabilities in school PE		**Separation of children with disabilities in school PE**	
Advantages	**Disadvantages**	**Advantages**	**Disadvantages**
Increases awareness	Could lead to bullying	Specialist teachers focus on specific needs	Can reinforce feeling of being different
A more realistic reflection of society	Expensive and requires specialist teachers and resources	Specialist equipment more available	Reduces opportunities for disabled children to mix with able-bodied children and may make it harder to integrate later

Older people

- Why should young people and older people take part in regular physical exercise?
- Why do young people drop out of sport and older people often fail to give it another go?
- What can be done to improve the situation for these age groups?

Sport is good for older people because of the following.

- Health – strength, flexibility and overall well-being.
- Social reasons – self-confidence, enjoyment and friendships.
- Psychological reasons – as a focus and interest.

Why are older people not more involved in sport and physical recreation?	What can be done to improve the situation?
Low self-esteem – feeling that sport is for young people.	Educate, advertise, reinforce and encourage.
May be restricted physically, for example, comparative lack of flexibility, poor health.	Provide suitable activities at suitable levels, taught by specialist coaches/leaders. Encourage specialist advice to be sought about appropriate types and levels of activity.
Perception that they are not good enough.	Continue to educate at all levels on the benefits of lifetime sport.
Lack of choice with some facilities offering inappropriate or unappealing activities.	Ask what is wanted and provide a variety of taster sessions.
Lack of suitable or sufficient role models, media focus and information.	Get items in local newspapers and campaign for media coverage of veterans sports events.
Limited funds.	Reduced/subsidized entrance rates.
Lack of access and/or transport.	Provision of transport. Ensure that new centres are located in areas on good routes.
Poor experience of PE at school.	Re-educate about the image of sport and physical activity.
Leaders and coaches not specialized in working with older people.	Provide training and education for coaches and leaders.

Young people

Many of the points made above about participation by older people can be adapted to answer questions about young people. For example, reasons for young people dropping out of sport include:

- perception that you have to be good
- lack of transport unless by parents
- expense
- friends do not participate
- reduced opportunities at school because of constraints on school sport and PE departments
- lack of provision at recreative level.

CHECK !

Go back to the overview diagrams on pp. 93 and 120. If you are satisfied with your knowledge and understanding, tick off the sections that you have revised so far. If you are not satisfied, then revisit those sections and refer to the pages in the 'Need to know more?'

Exam practice

1 Explain the positive influences that each of the following can have on both mass participation and sporting excellence in the UK:

(a) UK Sport and home country organizations

(b) sports coach UK

(c) schools. (6 marks)

2 In what ways can the media influence sport? (4 marks)

3 'Sport cannot justify a drug culture.' Explain this statement in the context of cheating, risk to health, and role modelling. (5 marks)

4 Discuss the problems faced by wheelchair athletes in the UK in achieving excellence in sport. (5 marks)

Now go to p. 167 to check your answers.

Exam practice answers

You can see how you have done in all of the units you have studied by checking your answers here.

How did you do?

0–8 marks: Urgent! Spend more time on this section and try again.
9–14 marks: Not bad! Review the areas where you lost marks.
15–17 marks: Great! Review the areas where you lost marks.
18–20 marks: Fantastic! Go on!

Unit 1 Anatomy and physiology

Chapter 1 **Joints and movement**

Examination questions for joints and movement are incorporated within Chapter 2, 'Muscles and movement', as they would be in an examination.

Chapter 2 **Muscles and movement**

1 (a) 5 marks

1 mark for each answer

Joint	Joint type	Articulating bones	Movement produced	Prime mover
Spine	Cartilaginous/gliding	Vertebrae	*Flexion*	*Rectus abdominus*

Joint	Joint type	Articulating bones	Movement produced	Prime mover
Elbow	*Hinge*	*Radius, ulna, humerus*	*Flexion*	Biceps brachii

(b) 2 marks

2 marks from:

- *Eccentric*
- *Antagonist/lengthening but providing major force/negative work*
- *Acts as a brake*
- *Helps control movement*

(c) 3 marks

1 mark for type = fast glycolytic (Type IIb)

1 mark for structural characteristic from:	**1 mark for functional characteristic from:**
Size = large	*Force production = high*
Colour = white	*Relaxation time = fast*
Glycogen store = large	*Contraction speed = high*
Sarcoplasmic reticulum development = great	*Fatigue resistance = low*
Myelin sheath = thick	*Aerobic capacity = low*
Myosin ATPase activity = fats	*Anaerobic capacity = high*
Motor neurone size = large	
Fibres per motor neurone = many	
PC stores = large	
Mitochondria = few	
Capillaries = few	

2 (a) 3 marks

3 marks maximum, 1 for each of:

- *Joint type = ball and socket*
- *Articulating bones = humerus and scapula*
- *Agonist muscle = deltoid/latissimus dorsi/teres major/pectoralis major/triceps brachii*

(b) 4 marks

4 marks maximum, 1 for each feature and function (must have both structure and function)

Structural feature	Function
Shape of bones/ball and socket	*Movement/identifying types of movement*
Ligaments	*Hold joint in place/give stability*
Cartilage (hyaline/articular)	*Prevents wear and tear/reduces friction/shock absorber*
Muscles	*Provide strength/support/movement*
Synovial fluid	*Lubricates the joint*
Pads of fat	*Absorb shock/protect from wear and tear*
Bursae (sacs containing synovial fluid)	*Helps reduce friction/prevent wear and tear*
Menisci/articular discs	*Stabilize joint/act as shock absorber*
Articular/joint capsule	*Increase stability*
Synovial membrane	*Encloses joint and secretes synovial fluid*

3 3 marks

3 marks maximum, 1 mark each for:

- *Joint type = ball and socket*
- *Articulating bones = (head of) femur with (acetabulum/acetabular fossa) pelvic girdle/ilium/pelvis*
- *Prime mover = gluteus maximus/biceps femoris/semimembranosus/semitendinosus/gluteus medius (not hamstrings)*

Chapter 3 **Mechanics, motion and movement**

1 3 marks

3 marks maximum (must apply to practical example)

- *Size:*
  The larger the force, the further the object will travel, for example, a netball player can throw a ball further by applying more force.
- *Direction:*
  If a force is applied through the centre of gravity, the object will travel in the same direction as the force, for example, to kick a

ball in a straight line, the player must kick the ball through the middle (centre of gravity) of the ball.

- *Position of application:*
  If a force is applied off-centre, then angular motion will occur, for example, kicking a football on the side will create swerve/curl/ spin.

2 3 marks

3 marks, 1 mark each for:

- *First Law of Inertia – the athlete will remain stationary unless he/she applies a force, for example, sprinter remains in blocks until a force is applied.*
- *Second Law of Acceleration – the athlete must bend their legs to stop at the end of a routine/more force applied to the blocks or against the floor will cause greater acceleration/momentum is increased by swinging the arms at take off during a jump.*
- *Third Law of Reaction – when an athlete starts a sprint race, they drive against the blocks and the blocks drive back against the athlete.*

3 4 marks

4 marks for four from:

- *First Law – movement will only occur if force is applied, for example, a sprinter remains in the blocks until a force is applied to the blocks.*
- *Second Law – force = mass × acceleration/size of the force/ greater force will move object greater distance, for example, a sprinter will mover further and faster out of the blocks the more force he/she applies.*
- *Third Law – for every action there is an equal and opposite reaction, for example, take off at long jump. Performer pushes into floor and floor pushes back (reaction force).*
- *Direction of force/force applied through centre of mass increases the distance, for example, a long jumper will achieve a greater distance if force is applied through the centre of gravity of the body.*
- *Position of application of force/applying force off-centre will cause angular movement (spin).*

4 3 marks

3 marks maximum, 1 mark each from:

- *Headstand is easier to hold because of larger base of support.*
- *Headstand is easier to hold because of the three points of balance/wider base of support/handstand less stable because it only has two points of balance/narrow base of support.*
- *Centre of mass is lower in headstand, therefore more stable.*
- *Centre of mass over base of support.*
- *If centre of mass moves out of base of support, balance is lost.*

Chapter 4: Part I: **Cardiovascular system**

1 (a) 4 marks

4 marks maximum from graph showing:

- *Resting heart rate around 40–80 beats per minute*
- *Rise in heart rate prior to exercise/anticipatory rise*
- *Steep rise in heart rate at beginning of exercise*
- *Plateau during exercise (115–180 beats per minute range)*
- *Initial fast fall in heart rate during recovery*
- *Followed by gradual decline to rest*

(b) 2 marks

2 marks maximum:

- *Adrenalin is released*
- *Stimulates SA node*
- *Increases heart rate*
- *Also increases strength of contraction/stroke volume*

2 (a) 3 marks

3 marks maximum:

- *Baroreceptors – blood pressure, chemoreceptors – muscle chemistry*
- *Cardiac centre/medulla oblongata controls heart rate/sends impulse*
- *Autonomic control/nervous system (ANS)*
- *Impulses sent via cardiac accelerator nerve*
- *SA node is stimulated*
- *Known as sympathetic control*
- *Impulses sent via vagus nerve*
- *Known as parasympathetic control*

(b) 4 marks

4 marks maximum, 3 marks maximum for each phase:

- *Diastole:*
  - *The atria/ventricles are relaxed*
  - *Diastole phase lasts 0.5 seconds/semilunar valves closed*
  - *Blood flows into right and left atrium*
  - *Via pulmonary vein and vena cava*
  - *Pressure rises and forces blood into ventricles*
  - *Through AV valves/bicuspid and tricuspid valves*
- *Systole:*
  - *The atria contract, forcing the blood into the ventricles/atrial systole*
  - *The ventricles contract/ventricular systole*
  - *Bicuspid and tricuspid valves/AV valves shut to prevent backflow of blood*
  - *Blood forced through aorta/pulmonary artery*
  - *Semilunar valves forced open*
  - *Systole phase lasts 0.3 seconds*

3 (a) 3 marks

3 marks maximum, 1 mark each for:

- *Heart rate = the number of times the heart beats in one minute*
- *Stroke volume = the volume of blood pumped by each ventricle/the heart in one contraction*
- *Cardiac output = the volume of blood pumped by each ventricle/the heart in one minute/stroke volume × heart rate/Q = SV × HR*

(b) 4 marks

4 marks for four from:

- *Impulse initiates from SA node (sinoatrial node)/pacemaker*
- *This causes atrial systole/blood ejected out of right/left atrium*
- *Impulse received by atrialventricular node (AV node)*
- *Conducted down bundle of his/purkinje fibres*
- *Causes ventricular systole from apex of heart/blood ejected from right ventricles*
- *Heart passes into relaxation phase/diastole*
- *Allows atria to refill with blood*

Chapter 4: Part II: **Control of blood supply**

1 (a) 3 marks

Three marks for labelling two areas correctly:

- *Aorta – leaving heart and travelling to body*
- *Vena cava – from body to heart (RA)*
- *Pulmonary artery – leaving heart (RV) to lungs*
- *Pulmonary vein – leaving lungs to heart (LA)*
- *Heart correctly labelled*
- *Oxygenated blood and deoxygenated blood identified*
- *Blood vessels labelled (must have three) arteries, arterioles, capillaries, venules, veins*

(b) 2 marks

2 marks from the following:

- *Skeletal muscle pump/muscles contract to squeeze blood back to the heart*
- *Valves/direct blood flow back to the heart*
- *Respiratory pump/changes in pressure around abdominal cavity squeeze blood back to the heart*
- *Blood above the heart assisted by gravity*
- *Venoconstriction of veins returning blood to heart*
- *Blood vessels within organs vasoconstrict/pre-capillary sphincters constrict at organs*
- *Redistribution of blood flow from organs to muscles/vascular shunt*

2 (a) 2 marks

2 marks maximum from:

- *Flushes out lactic acid/waste products*
- *Keeps capillaries dilated/maintains blood flow/oxygen to muscles/reduces oxygen debt*
- *Maintains skeletal muscle pump/respiratory pump*
- *Prevents blood pooling*
- *Maintains venous return*
- *Maintains stroke volume/cardiac output/Q*
- *Maintains blood pressure*

(b) 2 marks

2 marks for two from:

- *(Vaso) dilation of blood vessels/opening pre-capillary sphincters*
- *Increases blood flow/oxygen to (working) muscles*

- *(Vaso) constriction of blood vessels to other organs/closing pre-capillary sphincters*
- *Vascular shunt*
- *An increase in muscle temperature results in oxygen dissociating from haemoglobin more readily*
- *Increase in temperature reduces blood viscosity (therefore blood flow improved)*

(c) 2 marks

2 marks from:

- *Dissolves in the plasma*
- *Combines with haemoglobin*
- *To form oxyhaemoglobin*

3 (a) 2 marks

2 marks for two from:

- *Greater volume of blood returned to heart*
- *EDV determined by VR*
- *SV/Q is dependent upon VR*
- *Therefore greater VR will increase SV*
- *A larger SV will increase Q*
- *Good VR maintains blood pressure*
- *Therefore more blood/O_2 supplied to the working muscles/increases aerobic performance*

(b) 4 marks

2 marks for two from:

- *7 per cent dissolved in/carried in the plasma*
- *23 per cent combines with haemoglobin/forms carbamonohaemoglobin*
- *70 per cent dissolved in water/forms carbonic acid/ forms H_2CO_3*
- *In plasma, dissociates to hydrogen ions/bicarbonate ions*

2 marks for four from: (not lactic acid)

- *Carbon dioxide alters acidity of blood*
- *Chemoreceptors detect change*
- *Alert control centre in medulla oblongata (CCC/RCC/MCC)*
- *Increase in HR/cardiac output/stroke volume*
- *Increase in (rate and depth) breathing/take more O_2 into body*
- *Control via muscular shunt*
- *More oxygen supplied to muscles*
- *Causes Bohr effect/more O_2 dissociates from haemoglobin*

(c) 3 marks

3 marks maximum, two from:

- *Mechanisms*
  - *(Vaso) dilation of arteries/arterioles supplying working muscles/vascular shunt*
  - *(Vaso) constriction of arteries/arterioles supplying/non-working muscles/non-essential organs, for example, tract, kidneys, stomach*
  - *Opening of pre-capillary sphincters supplying working muscles*
  - *Closing of pre-capillary sphincters supplying non-essential organs*
- *One mark from why*
  - *Blood is distributed away from non-essential organs where not required*
  - *Blood is directed to working muscles due to increased demand for oxygen*

Chapter 5 **Respiratory system**

1 (a)(b)(c) 3 marks

1 mark each for:

(a) Increase

(b) Decrease

(c) Decrease

2 2 marks

2 marks maximum, 1 each from:

- *Partial pressure O_2 reduced*
- *Reduction in diffusion gradient occurs*
- *Haemoglobin saturation depends upon PPO_2*
- *Haemoglobin not fully saturated*
- *Less O_2 is carried in the blood*
- *Therefore less O_2 available to muscles*
- *Fatigue sets in quicker*
- *Hyperventilation/breathing rate increases*

3 3 marks

3 marks maximum (2 marks maximum from each area):

- *How exchanged*
  - *Gas flows from area of high pressure to low pressure*

- *Partial pressure of oxygen is higher in the lungs/alveoli*
- *Partial pressure of oxygen is lower in the blood*
- *During exercise, there is a greater pressure/concentration/diffusion gradient*

- *Why beneficial*
  - *So faster diffusion will occur*
  - *More oxygen diffuses (down the diffusion gradient) into the blood*
  - *More oxygen is supplied to muscles*
  - *More oxygen means less anaerobic work/decrease in lactic acid/delaying muscular fatigue/OBLA*

4 2 marks

2 marks maximum, for 2 from:

Structure	Reason
Many alveoli/large surface area	Large amount of gas exchanged
Moist lining dissolving	Quick diffusion through
Walls one cell thick/short diffusion	Quicker diffusion path
Elastic walls	Larger surface area for diffusion/greater volume of air ventilated
Pleural membranes	Friction-free movement
Large blood supply/capillary network	Large amount of gas exchanged

5 (a) 2 marks

2 marks for 2 from:

- *Inspiration*
  - *External intercostals contract with more force*
  - *Diaphragm contracts/flattens*
  - *More muscles involved, trapezius/scalenes/sternocleidomastoid/pectoralis minor*
  - *Lift thoracic cavity further up and out/ribs move further upwards and outwards*
  - *Increases volume of cavity/decreases pressure/increases volume inspired*

(b) 3 marks

3 marks maximum, 2 marks maximum for how from:

- *Oxygen is transported by haemoglobin/oxyhaemoglobin*
- *Gas diffuses from an area of high pressure to an area of low pressure/high partial pressure of oxygen (PO_2) in blood/low PO_2 in muscle*
- *O_2 diffuses into the muscle*
- *Decreased PO_2 in muscle cell, which increases diffusion gradient/concentration gradient*
- *High partial pressure of carbon dioxide (PCO_2) in tissues/low PCO_2 in blood so CO_2 from haemoglobin*
- *Increase in temperature encourages greater release of O_2 from haemoglobin*
- *Bohr effect/increase in acidity/lower pH of blood allows greater release of O_2 from haemoglobin*
- *Increase in carbon dioxide in blood results in greater release of O_2 from haemoglobin*
- *Myoglobin has higher affinity for oxygen than haemoglobin*
- *Myoglobin is used to transport more oxygen to mitochondria*

2 marks maximum for beneficial from:

- *Increased supply of oxygen to (working) muscles*
- *Therefore more energy provided (ATO resynthesized)*
- *Removal of greater quantities of carbon dioxide/waste products*
- *Therefore increased heart rate/breathing rate*
- *Lowers acidity level/increases pH, which prevents early fatigue/increases endurance*

6 (a) 2 marks

2 marks maximum, 1 mark each for:

- *At rest – 4000/15,000 ml/min (4/15 l/min)*
- *Maximal – 100,000/180,000 ml/min (100/180 l/min)*

(b) 3 marks

3 marks maximum, 2 marks maximum for how control is exerted from:

- *Change in pH of blood (detected by chemoreceptors)/drop in oxygen tension*
- *Proprioreceptors (in muscles) detect movement*
- *Blood pressure changes (detected by baroreceptors)*
- *Emotional influences/lung stretch receptors*
- *Information received by respiratory centre (in medulla oblongata)*

- *Rate and depth of breathing regulated by (apneustix and pneumotaxic) inspiratory and expiratory centres*
- *Which sends nerve impulses to the respiratory muscles (via phrenic/intercostals nerves)*
- *These increase the rate and the depth of breathing*

2 marks maximum for why from:

- *Large volume of air expired more rapidly therefore more carbon dioxide expelled*
- *Large volume of air inspired therefore greater amounts of oxygen available*

Unit 2 Movement skills

Chapter 6 **Defining, developing and classifying skills in PE**

1 (a) (b) (c) 3 marks

3 marks maximum, 1 mark each for:

(a) Tennis player is able to get the ball into the service box on almost every attempt

(b) A gymnast performs a cartwheel in a fluent/controlled way/makes it look easy/effortless/minimum outlay of time, energy or both/ good technique/well co-ordinated

(c) A hockey player has a clear aim when passing the ball to a team mate/predetermined

2 2 marks

2 marks maximum, 1 mark for description and 1 mark for example: Incoming information is interpreted/judged and used to form the basis of decision. For example, a football player sees team mate become available and judges how fast he is moving to help him decide when to release the ball.

3 2 marks

2 marks maximum, 1 mark each from each area (practical examples must be used):

- *Self-paced*
  - *Rate of the skill is controlled by the performer/performer decides when to begin the skill/performer is proactive*
  - *Generally more closed/habitual*

- *Externally paced*
  - *Skill is controlled by the environment or other people/ performer reacts to an external stimulus/reactive*
  - *Generally more open*

4 2 marks

2 marks maximum, 1 mark for each of:

- *Skills cannot always be classified specifically/skills have many different characteristics*
- *Allows for a range of points along a scale*

5 2 marks

The skill must be identified. 2 marks in total, the diagrams must be explained.

1 mark for one of:

- *Open – skill is different each time it is performed as the situation is different. Skill is adapted to the different circumstances*
- *Closed – skill does not need to take account of other performers or situations. Skill follows a pre-learned pattern of movement*

1 mark for one of:

- *Discrete – skill has an obvious start and finish*
- *Serial – skill is a series of discrete elements linked together*
- *Continuous – skill has no obvious start or finish, the end of one movement is the beginning of the next*

6 3 marks

3 marks maximum, 1 mark each from:

- *We are born with our abilities*
- *Ability can be enhanced through childhood experiences, for example, we play chasing games with our families*
- *We learn sprinting techniques in PE lessons/specific skills require specific abilities*
- *Practise of the skill occurs*
- *We use our natural speed and learned techniques in the long jump*

7 4 marks

4 marks maximum, 1 mark each from:

- *Learned/a skilful performance will have to be practised*

- *Efficient/there is no wasted time or energy/the movement is effortless/controlled/fluent/well timed*
- *Goal directed/the performer knows what is required to achieve a successful outcome/predetermined result*
- *Good technique/performer can repeatedly reproduce the correct movement*
- *Aesthetically pleasing/looks good to the eye*

8 2 marks

2 marks maximum, 1 mark each for:

- *Open – practise should reflect the changing circumstances of the skill/varied practise*
- *Closed – skills can be practised in a repetitive way/fixed practise*

Chapter 7 **Information processing**

1 (a) 2 marks

Explanation of stages must include a practical example.

1 mark for:

X = display – information contained within the physical environment, for example, opponents, ball, pitch, posts, crowd, coach.

1 mark for:

Y = feedback – intrinsic feedback via propriorecepters/kinaesthetic awareness/extrinsic feedback via external information/feedback from the result of the action, for example, the ball went into the net, the handstand was not balanced.

(b) 2 marks

2 marks maximum, 1 mark each from:

- *Short-term memory has limited capacity/only store five to nine items/only stores information for 30 seconds*
- *Selective attention only allows relevant information through/ reduces amount of information received by STM/discards or filters irrelevant information*
- *Brain operates as a single channel organ/bottleneck occurs when more than one item tries to pass through*
- *STM initiates movement therefore the quicker the relevant details enter the STM, the quicker the response*

2 3 marks

1 mark each for:

- *Reaction time = time from the onset of the stimulus to the start of the response*
- *Movement time = time from the start of the response to the end of the movement*
- *Response time = time from the onset of the stimulus to the end of the movement/response time = reaction time + movement time*

3 (a) 2 marks

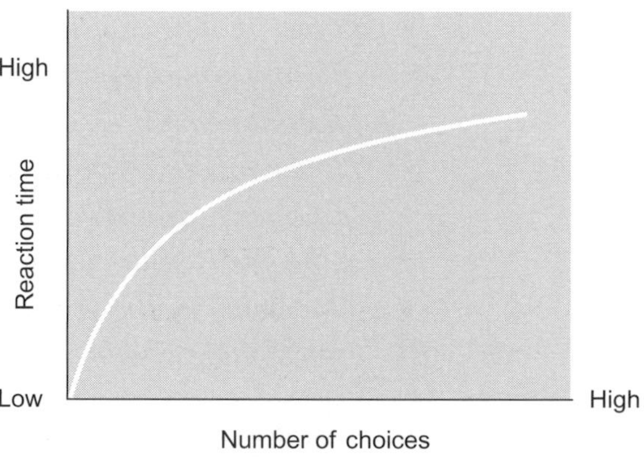

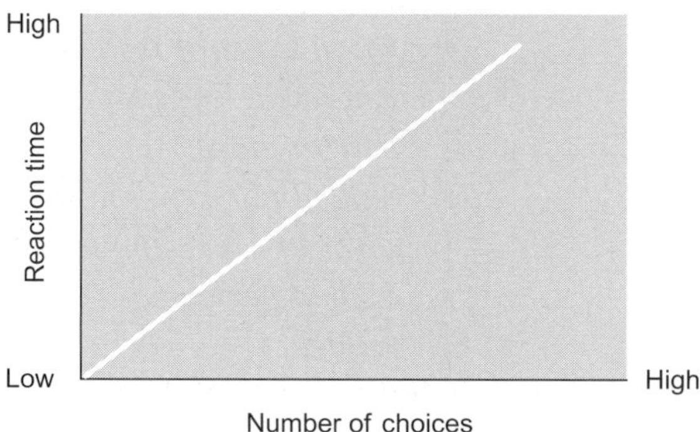

1 mark for correct labelling of axis, 1 mark for correct shape of graph

(b) 1 mark

1 mark for one of:

- *The more choices available, the slower the reaction time will be*
- *The more stimuli available, the slower the reaction*
- *The more response options, the slower the reaction*

4 4 marks

1 mark for each (must be in correct context/example) from:

- *Intensify the stimulus*
- *Increase selective attention/focussing*
- *Mental rehearsal*
- *Rehearse the response*
- *Use other transferable reaction experiences*

5 3 marks

1 mark each for:

- *Player moves as if to pass the ball to a team mate at his/her side (S1/first stimulus) and the opponent responds by following the fake movement (R1/first response)*
- *Player moves opposite way (S2/second stimulus) and the opponent cannot respond to this movement (S2/second stimulus) as he/she is still responding to first stimulus (S1)*
- *This delay in the second response (R2) is caused by a bottleneck effect/single channel hypothesis*

6 3 marks

1 mark each from:

- *Knowledge of results is essential for learning to take place*
- *Knowledge of performance – helps form picture of correct performance*
- *Skilled player – knowledge of performance – should come in the form of kinaesthetic feedback*
- *Skilled performer compares their performance to the perfect model*

Chapter 8 **Control of motor skill in PE**

1 1 mark

1 mark maximum, 1 mark from:

- *A motor programme is a set of generalized movements or sub-routines*
- *A pre-planned set of very specific muscle commands stored in the long-term memory*

2 4 marks

4 marks maximum, 1 mark each from:

- *A programme is created by repetition leading to a movement being grooved or over-learned*
- *A programme runs automatically following a decision and is retrieved from the long-term memory by short-term memory*
- *A motor programme is put into action by the effector mechanism*
- *Open loop (or memory trace) initiates the movement, whilst the closed loop (or perceptual trace) concludes it*
- *Motor programmes are operated by the dual action of open and closed loops*

3 (a), (b), (c), (d) 4 marks

1 mark each from:

- *Initial conditions – information about the environment, for example, position of the opponent and one's own position prior to passing a rugby ball*
- *Response specifications – what to do in the given situation, for example, the direction of the pass*
- *Sensory consequences – involves feel and any sensory information during the movement. This helps us to control the application of pressure, for example, how hard to pass*
- *Movement outcomes – concerns knowledge of results. The actual result, for example, the rugby pass has reached target*

4 3 marks

3 marks minimum, 1 mark each from:

- *A skill is taught as a whole if it is high organization and cannot be broken down into parts*
- *A simple skill such as cycling is best delivered as a whole*
- *A continuous skill, which appears to flow, such as sprinting, is best delivered by whole mode of practice*
- *If presented as a whole, the performer will more readily acquire the kinaesthesis or feeling tone of the skill*
- *A skill would be practiced as a whole if it required fast execution, for example dribbling a hockey ball*
- *In order to learn efficiently by this method, the performer needs to understand how the movement operates, for example, the swimmer may have a demonstration explained and experience the whole movement through use of a buoyancy aid*

5 4 marks

4 marks maximum, 1 mark each from:

- *The first sub-routine is taught and practised. The second is then added, both are practised together. A third sub-routine is taught and practised in isolation. All three are then joined together. For example: 1) A, 2) B, 3) AB, 4) C, 5) ABC*
- *Often used with serial skills, which are low in organization and easily broken down, for example, triple jump*
- *Used when skill is dangerous*
- *Triple jump (jumping phases) hop, step and jump could be taught by progressive part method*
- *Sub-routines are chained together*
- *Triple jump (or the skill you have named) is then performed as a whole unit*

6 4 marks

4 marks maximum, 1 mark each from:

- *Open loop involves a generalized series of movements or motor programmes, which are stored in the long-term memory*
- *The motor programme is triggered when required and activated by the movement effectors/one decision activates the programme/starts the skill*
- *The open loop is the memory trace*
- *Feedback cannot be used during the performance of the skill*
- *It explains how fast ballistic actions are performed, for example, a golf swing (once started, it cannot be adjusted)*
- *Feedback is gathered at the end of the skill, for example, drive was not straight*
- *Feedback can only be acted upon at the end of the movement and stored as a correction*

Chapter 9 **Learning skills in PE**

1 4 marks

4 marks maximum, 1 mark each from:

- *Cognitive learning theory states that learning is most effective when the whole problem is presented to the novice. For example, shooting during a basketball game*
- *It is a problem-solving approach to learning. The most successful outcome is discovered after a period of experimentation*

- *The problem can only be solved if the learner has a perception of the requirements*
- *The learner must use previous experience*
- *The self-esteem of the learner must be high to take on the problem*
- *The Gestaltian view states that adapting and conditioning games rather than perfecting a technique in isolation best accomplishes learning*
- *During problem-solving, there is often a latent period of unconscious thought. The solution may come suddenly. This 'flash' of thought when the solution is reached is called the 'eureka phenomenon'*

2 3 marks

3 marks maximum, 1 mark each from:

- *The cognitive phase of learning occurs at the novice stage*
- *The associative phase is the practise stage. The motor programme has at this stage been formed and the learner is aware of mistakes*
- *The autonomous stage is known as the expert phase. Actions are now automatic and performed with minimum conscious thought*
- *At the cognitive stage, extrinsic/external feedback should be given by the teacher. Provide knowledge of result/terminal feedback/ feedback should be positive*
- *The learner at the associative stage can start to use their own kinaesthetic or internal/intrinsic feedback (also called knowledge of performance) as the correct feeling tone will be developing. Knowledge of results is still important. Provide concurrent feedback when possible*
- *At the autonomous stage, internal feedback/knowledge of performance allows self-correction. Teacher can provide external feedback/knowledge of results. Apply negative feedback to finely tune the skill*

3 3 marks

3 marks maximum, 1 mark each from:

- *The S/R bond is the link or connection made by the performer between a response and a particular stimulus. The connection is sometimes called an association. For example, the starter's gun triggers the swimmer's movement at the beginning of a race*
- *The process of reinforcement increases the likelihood of behaviour re-occurring. A reinforcer can be positive or negative, but both serve to strengthen the learning bond*

- *Positive reinforcement is given after the desired behaviour has taken place, for example, the swimmer gains a badge for achieving a certain standard of proficiency. Therefore, a reward or show of approval is given to endorse behaviour*
- *Negative reinforcement involves withdrawing an adverse stimulus after desired behaviour has occurred in order to strengthen the S/R bond. For example, criticism will be withdrawn when the tumble turn is performed correctly*
- *Thorndyke's Law of Exercise states that if the task is repeated and reinforced, the learning bond will be further strengthened, whilst the Law of Readiness specifies that the participant must be mentally and physically capable of performing the task before reinforcement will facilitate learning*

4 3 marks

3 marks maximum, 1 mark each from:

- *Positive transfer occurs when one skill helps the learning and performance of another, for example, throwing transfers positively to tennis serving*
- *Negative transfer impedes the development of other skills, for example, a backhand shot in squash would be detrimental to its counterpart in tennis*
- *Retroactive transfer takes place when a newly learned skill facilitates or disrupts a previously learned skill, for example, a recently learned javelin throw would transfer to an earlier movement of a soccer throw in*
- *Proactive transfer takes place when old skills relate to a new skill*
- *Bilateral transfer is the transfer of learning from limb to limb, for example, a dominant right-footed player learning to kick with the left*

Be aware of other types of transfer, for example, intra-task transfer, near transfer and far transfer

5 3 marks

3 marks maximum, 1 mark each from:

- *Highlight the similarity between tasks and parts of tasks*
- *Develop practices, which would relate to the skill, for example, throwing relates to an overhead clear in badminton*
- *Skills that transfer negatively must not be taught as following options, for example, squash and tennis*

- *Complex tasks and those of high organization will benefit from 'task simplification', for example, short tennis replicates the conventional game*
- *Use the principles of one game to teach another, for example, soccer and hockey*
- *When using unequal transfer to make the task harder, the movement pattern must not be impeded, for example, pulling the weight in sprinting improves power but does it negatively influence the skill?*

6 4 marks

4 marks maximum, 1 mark each from:

- *When following a bowling demonstration in cricket, the learner must give attention to the model. The degree of attention is governed not only by the relevance of the skill but the status, competence and attractiveness of the demonstrator*
- *Attention must be guided to the key elements of the demonstration, for example, the straight bowling arm. The demonstration must be meaningful and create an impressive mental image, for example, the sideways body presentation of the bowler*
- *Retention refers to the length of time the learner can store the image of the demonstration. Storage is also aided mental rehearsal and visualization strategies, such as symbolic and creative imagery*
- *Motor reproduction is a vital sub-process in Bandura's model. The learner must have the ability and relevant experience to reproduce the skill of bowling*
- *The novice must be motivated to learn and keen to copy the demonstration*
- *External reinforcement of the model will increase the motivation of the copier*

Unit 3 Contemporary studies in PE

Chapter 10 **PE and sport in schools**

1 5 marks

5 marks maximum for five of the following (at least two from each section):

Sport as leisure	Sport as work
• *Amateur status*	• *Professional status*
• *Pursued voluntarily/for enjoyment*	• *Paid to participate/becomes a commitment*
• *Intrinsic reasons*	• *Extrinsic reasons*
• *In theory, 'sport for all'/should be available to all*	• *Selective/not everyone can do this*
• *Standard of performance not always important*	• *High standard of performance/quality of play essential to retain position*
• *Done in free time*	

2 6 marks

1 mark for identifying the value and 1 for the example.

Three from the following (with any suitable example):

- *Physical values, for example, cardiovascular fitness from athletics*
- *Preparation values, for example, learning and enjoying the lifetime sport of badminton*
- *Personal values, for example, developing leadership through being the captain of a team*
- *Qualitative values, for example, developing an appreciation of the quality of movements such as gymnastics*

3 4 marks

4 marks for four from:

- *To provide high quality teaching in PE and sport*
- *To increase opportunities for gifted and talented performers*
- *To give access to sports-specific qualifications*
- *To develop sporting opportunities in the community*
- *To link with local clubs*
- *To act as regional focal points for excellence in PE and sport*
- *To be focal points of the School Sport Co-ordinator programme*

4 5 marks

Credit must only be given for **one** *of the programmes (TOP sport or Dragon Sport).*

5 marks for any five from:

TOP Sport

- *Run jointly by Sport England/sportscotland/Sports Council for Northern Ireland and the YST*

- *Run in partnership with LEAs/schools/local authority Sports Development Officers/NGBs/Sports clubs*
- *Part of the TOPS programmes*
- *For seven to eleven year olds*
- *Supports the National Curriculum*
- *Provides sport-specific and age related equipment/equipment bags*
- *Provides illustrated resource cards*
- *Provides training for teachers*
- *Training provided by qualified trainers*

Dragon Sport

- *Supported by the YST*
- *Resources and training based on TOP Sport*
- *Aimed at seven to eleven year olds*
- *Aims to give a good sporting experience to youngsters*
- *Develops school/club links*
- *Supports clubs in developing junior sections*
- *Encourages involvement by parents, teachers and other adults*

Chapter 11 **Concepts of sport in society**

1 4 marks

4 marks for four from:

- *It has rules/a governing body*
- *It is competitive*
- *It needs commitment/dedication/determination/effort*
- *It needs skill*
- *It takes place at a specific time*
- *It takes place in a specific place/has set boundaries*
- *It is for personal satisfaction or for a job*
- *It involves fair play*

2 3 marks

You must point out the contrast/say how they are ***different*** *to get 1 mark.*

Tennis as recreation	Tennis as sport
Time flexible	*Fixed time limits/definite start times*
Space or location not fixed	*Space or location clearly defined*
NGB rules do not have to be used	*Strict rules*
Limited levels of competition	*Highly competitive*
Limited levels of skill and/or fitness/do not need to be good at it	*High skill and fitness levels*
Serious training/commitment not required	*High levels of training/ commitment required*
Not usually covered by media	*Can generate great media interest*
No sponsorship or funding evident	*Sponsorship and funding increasingly required to reach the top*

3 4 marks

4 marks for two from each section

Snooker should be classed as a sport because:	Snooker should not be classed as a sport because:
• *It is competitive/there are World Championships*	• *Snooker is not traditionally classed as a sport in this country*
• *Top performers are highly skillful*	• *Snooker is not physically strenuous*
• *Top level performers show great commitment*	• *Snooker is not part of the Olympic Games*

4 6 marks

1 mark for naming three levels and 1 for explaining each of them correctly.

- *Foundation – children learning basic movement skills/trying out lots of different activities/possibly through school PE programme*
- *Participation – youngsters choosing to take part in selected activities/for reasons of enjoyment/friendships/health and fitness/may be through extra-curricular school activities or via local sports centres or clubs*
- *Performance – commitment shown/serious training and coaching/formally organized activities at club or regional level/importance placed on improvement of standard*

- *Excellence – elite performers/representatives of country/fully committed individuals/possibly full-time performers*

5 3 marks

1 mark for each from:

- *Instructor – gives instructions, often about rules or safety/one-way communication, for example, when a swimming coach tells pupils that they must not walk on the poolside*
- *Trainer – gives advice on technique/training/is interested in performance/two-way communication increases as skill level of performer increases, for example, when a swimming coach does stroke analysis and correction*
- *Educator – concerned with the educational experience as well as the outcome or performance/a two-way relationship/the learner treated as an individual, for example, when a swimming coach gives opportunities for group work or reciprocal teaching/working with others*

Chapter 12 **Sport and culture**

1 6 marks

1 mark for naming a suitable example, for example, the Ashbourne football game/Gloucestershire cheese rolling, and 3 marks maximum for identifying characteristics.

Characteristics (3 marks maximum):

- *Local*
- *Occasional/annual*
- *Ritualistic*
- *Social occasions*
- *Rowdy/violent*

Reasons for survival (3 marks maximum):

- *Relative isolation of events*
- *A desire to retain tradition*
- *The importance as a social occasion (if not given above)*
- *A tourist attraction*

2 4 marks

1 mark for each identification and 1 for associated explanation.

The change	Explanation of the change
Military	*Guns were imposed – traditional weapons (and associated sports and pastimes) were restricted*
Commercial	*Independence of local community/need for hunting reduced when trade increased*
Christianity	*Brought by missionaries which reduced ritual/ pagan festivals*
Education/schools	*English style schools (with associated English sports and games) reduced influence of local communities*
Law and order	*Status of headman reduced with imposition of new governor and a police force*

3 6 marks

3 marks for reasons for seeking sporting success and 3 marks for strategies for achieving it

Reasons for seeking sporting success	Strategies for achieving sporting success
Stability of country	*Countries select a limited number of sports to concentrate on*
Increased health consciousness of the nation	*They unequally fund the chosen sport/s in relation to others*
To improve the status of the country in the eyes of the rest of the world/nation building	*Role models are used to inspire youngsters*
With the military and police often organizing sport, and successful athletes often given token jobs in the army, police force or government, defence of the nation can be improved	*High profile Olympic sports are chosen*
Sport can integrate or bring a nation together	*Simple, inexpensive, low tech sports are chosen*

4 4 marks

4 marks for four (two for positive and two for negative) from:

Positive:

- *Government interest and involvement means high levels of funding, which leads to a strong support network of coaches, administrators, doctors, and so on*
- *High funding also means excellent facilities*
- *A keenness to attract big international competitions*

Negative:

- *Government interest and involvement can lead to a willingness to turn to drugs and deviance in order to gain success*
- *Athletes become 'political pawns'*
- *Young athletes can have their health compromised*

Chapter 13 **Sporting issues analysis**

1 (a), (b), (c) 6 marks

1 mark for each of the three named organizations' influence on excellence and 1 mark for each of their influence on mass participation

	Excellence	Mass participation
UK Sport	• *Involvement with UKSI network centres* • *'More Medals' aspect of World Class Performance programme* • *Runs doping control* • *Lottery distribution* • *Attracts major sporting events* • *Improves international profile/image*	• *World Class Performance programme/more people/ more places* • *Active communities/ increased activity in communities/ disadvantaged groups* • *Awards for all/funding of local facilities/resources (lottery funding)* • *Sport Action Zones – targeting socio-economic deprived areas* • *Sports Development Officers – encourage participation in sport-specific areas and range of sports*
sports coach UK	• *Runs 'High Performance' workshops/workshops for high level coaches* • *Works closely with BOA/British Paralympic Association/Home country sports councils*	• *Runs introductory workshops for new coaches/workshops for established coaches/works with governing bodies to provide coach education schemes* • *Awards available* • *Study packs for new coaches* • *Co-ordinates Coaching for Teachers initiative*
Schools	• *Sports College status for some schools/links with UKSI centres* • *Send students to trials* • *Appointment of School Sport Co-ordinators*	• *Sportsmark awards for some schools increasing levels of participation* • *Sports Colleges work in the community/work with primary schools/work with majority of pupils* • *Introduce students to local clubs* • *Introduction to concept of lifetimes port/educated about health benefits* • *Provision of leadership awards*

2 4 marks

4 marks for four from:

The media can affect the:

- *rules, for example, the tie break in tennis brought in to make the game more exciting and to avoid long, drawn out matches*
- *scheduling, for example, the men's marathon at Los Angeles Olympics was run at the hottest part of the day in compliance with the media moguls*
- *format of sport, for example, one-day cricket or floodlit cricket with multi-coloured strips*

It can:

- *produce role models, which influence participation and the development of excellence*
- *encourage participation, of perhaps minority sports or by minority groups if air time is given*
- *encourage occasional participation, for example, during Wimbledon fortnight*
- *generate income that in theory can be ploughed back into grass roots development*
- *create a positive or negative image of sports or particular performers, for example, by concentrating on the violence of ice hockey, untrue perceptions can be created*

3 5 marks

5 marks for five (at least one from each of the three sections) from:

Cheating

- *Drug taking is unfair – it breaks the written rules of sports participation*
- *It breaks the unwritten codes of sportsmanship and fair play*
- *Not everyone has access to such illegal aids to performance*

Risk to health

- *Drug taking can be addictive and limit or take life*
- *Heart disease and liver disorders are caused by drug abuse*
- *Growth can be suppressed*
- *Sexual and gynaecological problems can be caused*
- *Behaviour and moods are affected and altered*

Role modelling

- *It is a bad example to young people*
- *Others may be tempted to copy the deviant behaviour thinking it 'normal'*
- *It gives a bad image to sport and lowers its status*

4 5 marks

5 marks for any five of the following:

Opportunity

- *Cost or lack of investment, sponsorship and media support*
- *Fewer opportunities to join clubs*
- *Insufficient specialist coaches*
- *The added problems of gender, race and age discrimination*

Provision

- *Physical problems of access and lack of special ramps, and so on*
- *Lack of suitable transport*
- *Problems of access to changing facilities, restaurant and bars, and so on*

Esteem

- *Discrimination by others*
- *The self-fulfilling prophecy that people with disabilities cannot rather than can*
- *Restricting attitudes*

And

- *Lack of sufficient role models*
- *Lack of sufficient specialist equipment*
- *Lack of suitable competition*